THE
VOW
A LOVE STORY &
THE HOLOCAUST

by

Michael Ruskin

Michael

THE VOW

DEDICATION:

To my beloved parents, whose unwavering courage,

love and faith, exemplified the magnificence of the human Spirit. . .

TABLE OF CONTENTS

TABLE OF CONTENTS

ACKNOWLEDGEMENTS

Writing a book about my parents' lives was harder then I thought and more rewarding than I could ever have imagined. Their lives truly set an example for all of us on how to overcome our fears and struggles of life with courage, perseverance, hope, and faith. The completion of this book could not have been possible without the support of my dear friends, especially those who gave their valuable time and talent to take me across the finish line.

My deepest thanks and gratitude go to my dear friend and amazing Graphic Designer /Illustrator Patricia Dibona. She made my book come to life through her incredible book layout and design. She has taken my book to a level I never could have imagined, and I am eternally grateful.

A very special thanks is deserved to my editor, Trish Ruigh Scott for her insightful editing and valuable collaboration on keeping "the ship" steady through some rough waters. I greatly appreciate her support throughout this amazing journey.

To my dear friend Linda Love, who helped design the e-book back in 2011, which evolved into the book version. Her efforts are greatly appreciated.

To Francine Lowe and Reg Regenstein, who supported my efforts and introduced me to some amazing authors and professionals in the publishing field who offered valuable tools to enhance the book's content.

To Evan Lever in London, England, for his research in Lithuanian history and who planted the seeds to rewrite the e-book. And through his research introduced me to my two cousins who live here in the United States, who I never knew existed.

To Brad Jacobs in Los Angeles who also provided great inspiration to my efforts and offered other media suggestions to reach a wider audience.

ACKNOWLEDGEMENTS

To my cousin Shoshana Getler in Israel, who offered valuable input to my family's history and supported me with valuable photographs which are contained in the book.

To my dear, long-time friend Howard Cohen who connected me with some wonderful resources and supported my efforts throughout the book's creation. His friendship over the years will always be treasured.

And finally, to my Mother and Father who were with me every step of the way, as I documented their journey to keep their legacy alive. I felt their presence guiding me every day, especially during the late hours of the night when finding the right words did not come easily. I love both of you from the bottom of my heart for bringing me to the planet and knowing you are still here with me.

Michael

"*Give me your tired, your poor,*
your huddled masses
yearning to breathe free."

Emma Lazarus, 1883 on the Statue of Liberty

PHOTO CREDIT:
The Ruskin family photo album

PHOTO:
Photo taken by David Ruskin on a Ferry boat to Liberty Island. His wife and two sons were also on board on their first visit to meet Miss Liberty in 1954.

PROLOGUE

I want to begin by introducing myself and explaining why I wrote this book. As the son of Holocaust survivors, and the last surviving member of my immediate family, I felt compelled to write a biography of two amazing people I call my heroes, my parents, David and Dora Ruskin. Actually, they are heroes for all who believe in LOVE, FAITH, and the COURAGE to persevere. Although they departed this earth many years ago, they live in my heart every day for the love and guidance they gave my late brother and me.

As you read through these pages, you will see how their relationship blossomed and how their love transcended the evil of one man, Adolf Hitler, and those who followed him. Please, don't let the title of this book mislead you. My intention was not to make the Holocaust the focal point of the book, for it is a love story. But it does offer a sharp contrast between the horrific atrocities unleashed by the Nazi Regime, and the extraordinary bond of two people whose only goal was to survive. Within the larger context, the book differentiates between love and hate, hope and fear, life and death. Describing one without the other would have greatly diminished the message this book was meant to convey.

It is my sincere hope that future generations will recognize the importance of this book which demonstrates how blatant discrimination, hatred and hostility against innocent people can overtake a country, leading to the death of millions of human beings. For without understanding how such a misguided ideology as Fascism could take root in a country such as Germany, whose culture and history were so lauded, we are destined to repeat the past. This is true whether such hatred is against a nationality, a religion or a culture.

It is with respect and love that I dedicate this book to my father and mother and millions of the "Innocent" who had the courage to stand up for freedom and who shined a light on an ideology which had no place among civilized nations. I further wish to extend my deepest gratitude and thanks to the United States Armed Forces, the Allies and Partisans who bravely fought and died to liberate tens of millions of people from the tyranny that spread throughout the European continent.

THE VOW

This book is based on historical fact and the lives of my parents, who, on very rare occurrences shared with me their experiences during the Nazi occupation of Lithuania. As bits and pieces of their past came forth, I was still too young to fully comprehend the magnitude of their profound horror and pain growing up in their home country of Lithuania. Even the country was a place I knew very little about. All I remember growing up was that Lithuania was located in Eastern Europe near the Russian border, and my ancestors originated from that region of the world. I could safely say that even today, there are many people in the West who would have a difficult time finding Lithuania on a map.

It was many years later before I began to fully understand the geography, the people and the events which led up to World War II and my parents' horrific experiences. Sadly, by the time I came to this realization, my father had already passed and my mother was in a nursing home with Alzheimer's disease. It was in the fall of 1993 that my journey really began to uncover the details of their incredible journey together, and it came to me by sheer accident …. Or perhaps it didn't.

It was late one night, a few days after my father's funeral on September 23, 1993, when I decided to drive over to my parents' Miami Beach condominium to begin removing and packing many of my father's personal belongings. Since my mom was already in a nursing home, my brother and I felt it was time to begin preparing the sale of our parents' condo. I couldn't sleep that night due to my dad's passing, so I decided to straighten up the Unit before the real estate broker arrived the next morning.

As I was removing odds and ends from my father's bedroom nightstand, I came across an unmarked folder buried beneath unopened envelopes, old bills and magazines. The folder appeared to be pushed to the back of the lower drawer, as if "Pop" (my dad) was trying to hide the contents from being discovered. As I opened the tattered folder I saw a considerable number of weathered documents and correspondence written in both English and German. I soon realized that most of the material pertained to my parents' physical and mental condition after the war. There was also a detailed accounting of the events that took place while my parents were still in captivity inside the ghetto in Kaunas, Lithuania (1941-44) as well as the Dachau and Stuttoff concentration camps (1944-45). Much of the information I came across was prepared by New York physicians and was written in the early 1960's. Some of the papers were testimonies my parents gave to the doctors describing the atrocities that were inflicted upon them during World War II and the Holocaust. The material evidently was a draft that was used to petition the German courts in Munich for reparations for the suffering and loss they endured during the war.

As I read through the material, my heart sank. The information was both heartbreaking and shocking, as the doctors described in detail the horrific events during the Holocaust. It left me cold. Other letters included release papers from the Kauen Concentration Camp where my father was detained before being transferred to Dachau, and papers from the UN Refugee Committee and Red Cross International, pertaining to my parents' liberation. I was totally unprepared for what I was reading. As I sat there visualizing the images from the description of their experiences, I realized how incredibly difficult it must have been for them to recount their past, not to mention to repress their ordeal for years in order to raise a family. It was very late when I left their condo that evening and of course I took the folder with me. I never said a word to anyone, other than my brother.

Fast-forward to 2011. My mom passed in 2002 and I was now living in Roswell, Georgia. As I was going through my desk drawer one day, after having recently moved, I came across my parents' folder again. For so long I had pushed the information I found in '93 to the back of my mind. I really didn't give the information much thought, as I tried to rationalize their experiences were now all in the past. In any case, my parents were no longer alive. I don't remember what possessed me that day, but I decided to write their biography in an E-book which was published online in 2011. I also donated the original documents that I found in 1993 to the Holocaust Museum Library in Washington, D.C. Why I waited so long to write their biography is still unclear to me. I suspect the topic was too difficult for me to handle at the time or God had different plans for me. I, nevertheless do know that finding my parents' testimonies was the catalyst for both the original e-book and the book you are about to read.

I believe through these pages you will be inspired by the underlying message my parents were sending through their relationship together. This is their life story, their legacy. I only stand in their place to bring forth and honor their experiences with the rest of the world.

In order to begin connecting the dots to develop a cohesive narrative, I conducted extensive research utilizing multiple sources on the history of Lithuania leading up to World War II. Additional information was obtained from the Holocaust Museum Library in Washington, D.C.; Yad Vashem Museum in Jerusalem, Israel; and other sources. Just as important were my conversations with my cousin in Tel Aviv, Israel, and historical information I received from an independent researcher on Lithuanian Jewish history.

As I continued my research to the backdrop of my parent's early lives in Lithuania, I was shocked to learn of the sheer devastation, suffering and death of the Jewish people which occurred in eastern Europe (Latvia, Estonia, and Lithuania) before and during the Nazi occupation, which included Russian occupation, before 1941. The country of Lithuania was "ground zero" for the death of Jews on a percentage basis among all European countries from 1938 to 1945. Of approximately 208,000–210,000 Jews living in Lithuania, an estimated 190,000–195,000 were murdered before the end of World War II, most between June and December 1941. An astonishing 95% of Lithuania 'Jews were massacred over the three year German occupation. More deaths in a percentage basis than any other country during the entire war. In total, the number of Jews murdered during the Holocaust throughout Europe between 1938 -1945 totaled 5,594,623 out of a Jewish population of 9,689.500, or a 57.7 percentage. (1,2)

This staggering statistic made it even more compelling for me to write this book, especially when you realize that BOTH my mother and father survived against such odds. Their survival was nothing short of a miracle.

My parent's journey began when they were still in their early 20's, after the Nazi party's rise to power. This was a time when Adolf Hitler and his "brown shirt hedgemen" roamed the streets of Munich, Germany, to intimidate the Jewish residents with Nazi propaganda and promote pan-Germanism, anti-Semitism, and anti-Communism. Hitler would frequently denounced international capitalism and communism as part of a world-wide Jewish conspiracy. At the time, the rest of Europe was only giving Hitler passing interest, since most believed he was a "crack-pot" who would be contained within the borders of Germany. And he certainly wasn't thought of as a threat to the entire European continent, or the world for that matter. But I digress …Now let me introduce you to my beloved parents and their story which very few people ever knew....until now.

PROLOGUE

FOOTNOTES:

1 Bubnys, Arūnas (2004). "Holocaust in Lithuania: An Outline of the Major Stages and Their Results". *The Vanished World of Lithuanian Jews. Rodopi.* pp. 218–219. ISBN 978-90-420-0850-2.

2 Wikipedia – The Holocaust in Lithuania Destruction of Jewry: Creative Attribution share alike license.

Dora

Dora

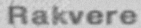

CHAPTER 1
THE EARLY YEARS

"There is nothing like a dream, to create your future."

Victor Hugo

DATELINE: LITHUANIA – 1915 - 1935

PHOTO SPREAD:
Dora and family, including sisters and nephews/nieces. Not all family members are present. Dora is in the upper far right in the photo. The photo includes the family's housekeeper, Norma, (center).

PHOTO:
Rabbi Kekst, with wife, Chaja and some of the family. Dora is in the upper right. Not all family members are present.

PHOTO CREDIT:
The Ruskin family photo album

CHAPTER 1
THE EARLY YEARS

"There is nothing like a dream, to create your future."

Victor Hugo

DATELINE: LITHUANIA – 1915 - 1935

DORA RUSKIN:

Dora Kekst was born August 15, 1918 in Mazeikiai, Lithuania, a village on the banks of the Venta River, northwest of the capital city of Kaunas, Lithuania. The village's population included farmers, merchants and people of various trades. The town was comprised of a community bank, a few grocery stores, several churches and a synagogue, as well as a central railway station which connected Mazeikiai to Kaunas and surrounding communities. With grassy rolling hills and sprawling farmland, Mazeikiai had a pastoral beauty which drew people from across the region. Cold, snowy winters melted into beautiful springs and summers, which brought out many of the residents to bicycle or picnic on the lush grassy hills of the countryside, or to swim in the freshwater lakes nearby.

While there was little intermingling between Jews and Gentiles, there was a respectful coexistence. The merchants from the town served surrounding communities and residents of neighboring Latvia, who frequently crossed the border to shop in Mazeikiai on weekends. Just on the outskirts of town, among the rolling hills, was the residence of Rabbi Chaim Kekst and his wife Chaja, along with their nine children. There were six girls- Dora, Ashira, Ruchana, Sara, Riva, and Bela; and three boys- Abraham, Joseph, and David. The Rabbi was the spiritual leader in the local synagogue and was very well known in the Jewish community. He was highly respected for his kindness and wise counsel. His sermons emphasized at each Sabbath Service that it was the responsibility of every Jew to live a pious life by obeying the Ten Commandments and following Jewish tradition and culture. He would close each sermon with: "We are all our brother's keeper and must treat everyone with kindness and love, regardless of their faith or background." Rabbi Kekst came from a long line of rabbinic scholars, and this was also the message that had been passed down from one generation to the next.

As would be expected, the Kekst children were raised in a very traditional Jewish home. The children were close, but still had their share of disagreements, sibling rivalries and varied interests, as most families do. The longtime family housekeeper, Norma, kept the children in line, making sure they did their homework, kept their rooms neat, and did their chores. Never married, She loved the children as if they were her own, but she believed in discipline. Although the children would complain about her rules from time to time, they still loved her, for they knew the rules originated from their father. Norma was considered as part of the family and the children depended on her for giving them sound advice and encouragement. She would always say to them, "make your parents proud of you." They were raised to be a reflection of their parents, with high morals, humility, and a kind heart for everyone.

The Kekst family residence was situated on prime farmland and there was always a lot to do to keep the farm well-maintained. There were animals to feed, a barn to clean, crops to tend, and repairs to make, which mostly fell upon the children. It was not unusual to see the children painting the barn when needed, mending fences along the outer pasture or milking the cows. The Rabbi felt that chores taught them responsibility and to understand that life can be hard, but the children took it in stride and it was for the good of the family.

Growing up, the children were all good students. Two of the boys entered rabbinic study, following in the footsteps of previous generations. The youngest son, Abraham, a mathematics prodigy, and hoped to study engineering, which pleased his father immensely. The girls were ambitious as well. Dora and Sara aspired to become elementary school teachers, while the other four girls planned careers in nursing or related services to help the community. All participated in extracurricular school activities, such as soccer, drama clubs, and Bible classes at the synagogue. The Rabbi and his wife were proud of their children, who they expected to be model citizens of the community, Jew or Gentile.

The Rabbi was widely considered to be a kind and generous man. He offered guidance and support to anyone who sought his advice, regardless of their circumstances. Occasionally, the Rabbi would open his home to people who recently lost their jobs, and offered them work on the farm until they got back on their feet. By the time Dora was in high school, the Great Depression was affecting Europe, and times were hard. The Rabbi on occasion gave fresh vegetables and fresh milk from his prize cows to the needy, who were always grateful for the Rabbi's generosity.

Coming from a Rabbinic family and having studied Torah since childhood, Rabbi Kekst was considered a scholar of Jewish literature, philosophy and scripture. Many would come to his home for advice or to talk about Bible interpretation, which was his favorite topic. Each Sabbath his synagogue was well attended and his sermons were always inspirational. The congregation looked forward to the Sabbath for they knew the Rabbi would always bring up stories which many in the congregation could embrace, and his words were always comforting.

As a child, Dora was precocious, smart, strong, and self-willed. Conformity didn't come easy for young Dora, but Norma made sure she always fell in-line. On occasion, she tested the norms of their conservative Jewish home by staying out later than allowed, or going to movies that her parents frowned upon. She was very popular among her friends and an excellent student at school. She was known for her quick mind, vivid imagination and a knack for speaking various languages at a very young age, which impressed even her teachers. As she entered into her final years in high school she became an incurable romantic and sometimes dreamed of becoming a famous movie actress. She was an avid movie buff, with her favorite actress being Ingrid Bergman. She knew that becoming a movie star was just a pipe dream, since her parents expected more of her considering she was the rabbi's daughter. So instead, she relished performing in school plays, where audiences gave her standing ovations for many of her performances.

Dora had a sweet personality and was strong willed, a combination which ingratiated her to her father. What annoyed her father, however, was when Dora was late for dinner, especially on Fridays, when the family observed the Sabbath at sundown. For the Kekst household, Friday evenings were a time for the family to come together in reflection, prayer, and conversation around the dinner table.

One Friday night, Dora arrived home late from school and had no excuse. Although she apologized profusely to her parents and her siblings, her father had reached his limit of accepting her excuses and apologies. She and was sent to her room without dinner. The next morning before breakfast Dora was taken aside by her Mother and said, "Dora, your father and I are very disappointed that you've been coming home late for dinner on Friday nights, knowing it's the beginning of Sabbath. We've decided that starting on Monday you are to come home directly from school and go straight to your room to study until dinner. We will let you know how long you will follow this schedule in a few weeks." Dora was devastated and had no response. She turned and walked away feeling totally dejected. At breakfast that morning she sat at the table pouting in silence as the family was chatting away about Sara's birthday party planned for the next day in the backyard. Norma, serving breakfast to the family, looked over at Dora and gave her a smile. Dora just sat there stone-faced looking straight ahead, not saying a word. After breakfast Dora slowly walked over to her Father who was still sitting at the table looking over his notes for his upcoming sermon. Dora approached him putting her arms on his shoulders, giving him a kiss. "Pop, I am so sorry about last night and I promise to never come home late again." The Rabbi looked up from his notes and just smiled. The following day Dora joined her siblings and her parents along with a number of classmates to celebrate Sara's birthday in the backyard. Dora seemed a bit more cheerful, celebrating the day with her family and their friends, but thoughts of her upcoming punishment were still in the back of her mind. As the party was coming to a close, her father walked over to Dora and said with a twinkle in his eyes, "Dora, your Mother and I have decided to accept your apologize, but this is the last time we will forgive you. No more being late, do you understand?" Dora, holding back her excitement, "yes Poppa, I promise." And she hugged him with a smile on her face. Dora always seemed to find a way to soften her Father's heart; they had a "special bond", which her sibling couldn't understand.

It was not long after Sara's birthday that a letter arrived stating that both Dora and Sara were accepted to attend the Teachers college in Kaunas, the capital city of Lithuania at the time. Despite the age difference between the sisters, Sara had skipped a grade so they were going off to college at the same time. The girls were ecstatic. This would be the first time they would be away from home and living in a bigger city. They're dream of becoming teachers was one step closer to becoming real. The summer of 1937 was a rather long one for the girls, as they counted the days to the beginning of classes and a new chapter in their lives. However. What was on the horizon was not a new chapter, but the beginning of an entirely "new book" that would change their lives forever . . .

DAVID RUSKIN:

David Ruskin (Duvid Ruksen at birth) was born May 27,1915, in the town of Kedainiai (Kedain in Yiddish), Lithuania, 50 miles north of Kaunas. Kedain was known for agriculture and dairy products, soybeans and corn.

David was born into a working-class family, who lived in a modest neighborhood on the south side of town. His parents, Meyer and Mina Ruskin ran a haberdashery, and lived upstairs in a small 3 room apartment. They sold custom dress gloves, hats, belts and scarves to the local residents. The store produced enough income to keep the family's bills paid, but during the summer months, when the need for gloves and winter clothing were off season, they had to conserve, while Meyer picked up odd jobs to make ends meet. Meyer, ran the store for nearly 10 years, along side his wife, Mina, when Meyer suddenly passed away from a heart attack. After his death, Mina had to take on the responsibility of running the small store by herself, with some help from her two children, David and his sister, Ruth. David, still in high school, helped in the store after school and on weekends, while Ruth, David's older sister, helped her mother with the bookkeeping and assisting customers. The Depression made it difficult to make ends meet, and they all worked hard, knowing the store was their only source of income.

While in high school, David excelled in sports, especially soccer. He spent hours practicing on the soccer field. Playing with the high school soccer team, he was known as someone who could kick goals from midfield, which drew the attention of coaches and players alike. During his senior year in high school, David was approached by his head coach to see if he would be interested in the tryouts for the Lithuanian National Soccer Team. Lithuania, known in past years to be one of the stronger countries in soccer at the Olympics, was planning to participate in the 1936 Olympic Games in Munich, Germany, only a few years away. Adolf Hitler, already in power in Germany, was touting German athletes as the greatest in the world, and were destined to win the Olympic games in 1936. David had always dreamed of representing his country in the Olympic Games, and now he thought he might have the opportunity to play for his native country alongside the best amateur soccer players in the world. That evening, after practice, David ran home to tell his mother the news about participating in the Olympic tryouts. His excitement was hard to contain, but after his conversation with his mom, he decided his dream would have to wait. He realized that leaving the store for such a long time would make it difficult for his mother and sister to run the business, especially with winter coming, they needed all the help they could get. Yet he never stopped thinking of what could have been.

After graduating high school, David continued working at the store with his mother and sister, but he knew he had no interest in spending the rest of his life selling accessories. He wanted to follow his real passion, to become an electrician. Since he was a little boy, David had always loved fixing things, especially electrical appliances and various types of electrical motors. He decided to enroll in a technical school after graduating from high school. Even in high school, he would approach residents in the neighborhood to offer his services to repair appliances or other electrical devices. People were amazed at David's ability to repair just about anything. He became known as the "Fix-it Boy".

As David was working hard at his side business, taking classes and helping out at the store, he had very little free time for himself. One day as he was on his way home from classes, Mr. Morrison, a man from a neighborhood, pulled up beside him in his truck. Mr. Morrison had been running a successful electrical contracting business in Kedain for many years. He was well known in the community, and his contracting business was always in demand among residents as well as businesses in town. Mr. Morrison had heard about David's side business from others in the community, and believed that David would have the skills to be of value to his company's business. After exchanging pleasantries, Mr. Morrison said, "I'm wondering if you would be interested in a job as an apprentice with my company, David? I have a need for someone with your skills, and based on what I'm hearing from some of my neighbors, you're pretty good." David, surprised by the offer, smiled, flattered by his comments. Mr. Morrison continued to discuss the projects he had in mind and the opportunity to grow with the company. David didn't hesitate, "Mr. Morrison this all sounds great, but I have to discuss this with my mom, and I will get back to you tomorrow." When David got home late that afternoon, he explained the meeting he had with Mr. Morrison and his job offer to his mother and sister. They all agreed that this would be a wonderful opportunity to gain experience and still help out at the store when he could. The following week, David began his new job with the Morrison Electrical Contracting Company of Kedain, as an apprentice. Over the next few months, Mina and Ruth ran the store most of the time, while David worked hard to prove himself in his trade. Mina and the children were deeply committed to each other as a family unit. She believed that their love for one another and God gave them the strength they needed during the hard times of the 1930's. She attributed their faith and closeness as a family directly to her late husband, Meyer. There were nights when Mina would lie in bed sobbing, wishing her husband was still alive so he could see how he helped to influence the children to be so devoted as a family unit. David reminded her of Meyer more and more with each passing year. As she was lying there in the darkness, she knew that the spirit of her husband would be with her forever.

David and his sister continued to work closely together, even though David was working many hours for Morrison as time went on. Yet as siblings, they had very different interests and aspirations. Ruth had an affinity for numbers, and enjoyed taking care of the bookkeeping and helping her Mother at the store. David, on the other hand, wanted to have his own electrical contracting business someday, and become a class A electrician.

In 1936, while still working for Morrison, David was called up for military service in the Lithuanian army reserve, serving two years of active military duty. During this time David was at the front lines fighting Poland in a land dispute which also brought the Soviet Union into the fray. Although he was wounded in the leg toward the end of his military service, he successfully completed his tour of duty, and returned home to find that he had lost his job at Morrison's company. Discouraged, he went back to his part-time handyman business, which was sporadic at best, and working at the family store again.

One day, after a long day at the store, David ran into one of his high school buddies who mentioned that he had heard there were plenty of good paying jobs in Kaunas, less than 50 miles from home. David was excited about the news since he had always wanted to move to a bigger city, where there was more opportunity to advance his trade and meet new people. The distance was perfect, too, since he could still come home occasionally to visit his mother and sister and support the shop when needed. Kaunas had recently become the capital of Lithuania, after the previous capital, Vilnius, was partitioned by the victors of World War I to the newly recreated Poland. After WW I, Kaunas went through a major transformation, incorporating surrounding suburbs and becoming the seat of government.

CHAPTER 1: THE EARLY YEARS

With increase urbanization, the population of the city increased by nearly 66%, from 92,000 to 153,000. Almost overnight, stately buildings had sprung up in the downtown area, along with new parks and a larger theatre district. As business boomed, many members of the Lithuanian "high society" moved into the inner city, including top politicians, army officers, artists, professional sports figures, as well as state government workers. Kaunas became the home of Lithuania's only international airport, with connecting flights throughout Europe.

The real estate market in Kaunas also was on an upswing, with housing and commercial buildings being built briskly to keep pace with the growing population and tourism. Kaunas was the perfect location for David to find work and improve his trade. So, in 1938, David packed his bags and headed to the train station for Kaunas. As he waved goodbye to his mother and sister at the railway platform, he was taken over by intense guilt for leaving. He prayed that his father would understand that he had a life to live and that he couldn't find it in Kedain. As he looked back to see them walk away in the distance, he closed in eyes as tears rolled down his face. There was no turning back now, he thought, as the train whistle rang out. He was riding a train to destiny. Yet, thoughts of his Mom and Sister back home lingered for a long time.

As the train pulled into Kaunas, he gazed out the window and saw a bustling city much larger than he had imagined, which gave him a bit of uncertainty on where he would begin his new adventure. Yet he was excited about the possibilities. He pushed ahead with his plan. He decided to first locate construction sites within the city to inquire about work. Since their was a shortage of good electrical technicians and electricians, it didn't take long for him to land a job at one of the larger buildings under construction in the business district. Next, he needed a place to live, which he found a few days later, not far from the work site, which was convenient. The following week, he contacted his mother and sister to tell them that he was working and had found a nice place to live and things were going well... At least for now.

CHAPTER 2

LIFE IN THE CAPITAL CITY

"Deep in my soul, I know that I'm your destiny."

Rven-Symone´

DATELINE: KAUNAS, LITHUANIA
1937 – 1940

PHOTO SPREAD:
CAPTION:
Dora

PHOTO SPREAD:
CAPTION:
Sara

PHOTO CREDIT
The Ruskin Family Photo Album

CHAPTER 2

LIFE IN THE CAPITAL CITY

"Deep in my soul, I know that I'm your destiny."
Rven-Symone´

DATELINE: Kaunas, Lithuania 1937 – 1940

Upon graduating from high school, Dora, along with her Sister Sara were accepted to a prestigious Teacher's College in Kaunas. Their parents couldn't have been more proud of their accomplishments. So in 1937, both young ladies were off to school to fulfill their dreams of becoming elementary school teachers. Kaunas, located 120 miles southeast of Mazeikai was experiencing unprecedented growth as more and more people were drawn to the faster pace lifestyle and the city's booming economy. People from all walks of life were taking up residence including leading doctors, lawyers, business professionals and entrepreneurs. All looking to make a name for themselves. Dora and Sara were excited about life in a bigger city, where the "energy" was a stark contrast to the agricultural community they grew up in. Further, the Sisters had two brothers (Joseph and David) who were also living in Kaunas, attending the Jewish seminary to become Rabbis. Having family close by made adjusting to "City" life much easier for the girls and also gave their parents reassurance that they would be watched over by their overly protective brothers.

Soon after the sisters arrived, they settled into a small two-bedroom apartment, and prepared for their first semester. Their days were kept busy studying, spending time with their brothers and exploring the attractions of the city. It was a happy time for Dora and

Sara, meeting new and interesting people, and having the freedom to live life, without the strict rules placed upon them when they were living at home.

As the first semester ended, the brothers decided to invite a small group of classmates and friends to their apartment to celebrate winter break. Dora and Sara and a few of their girlfriends from school joined the celebration. The apartment was small, but the mood was festive and the conversation was lively. All appeared to be relieved that the first semester was over and were looking forward to some downtime. Most of the conversations among the students were about classes, activities around the city and the best places to eat. Dora and Sara, being the "new kids on the block" were young, attractive and quite friendly and certainly not to be ignored, especially by one young man, Noah. Noah was a close friend of Dora's two brothers who met Noah at the local synagogue. A handsome, tall, well-spoken chemical engineering student from the technical college in town, he was introduced by Joseph to the two sisters. It didn't take long before Dora and Noah struck up a conversation. Having similar backgrounds and coming from a small rural farming community, they both soon realized how much they had in common. As the evening progressed, Dora found herself quite drawn to this ambitious, well-mannered young man who had a resemblance to her younger brother Abraham. Noah was smitten by Dora almost from the moment he saw her. There was a chemistry between them that was obvious to those in the room. They spent the rest of the evening talking about their families, growing up in a small rural community and their love of the movies. As the evening came to a close, the couple decided to meet again the following week for dinner.

As the weeks passed, their time together became more and more frequent, spending weekends sightseeing, strolling the parks of the city and enjoying dinner at posh restaurants around town. As their courtship continued to flourish. Their feelings grew. Feelings that frightened Dora at times, as she didn't have much experience dating. Nevertheless, she followed her heart, as did Noah.

Page 16

One evening, after dinner, they took a stroll by the river, near Dora's apartment. They soon found a park bench facing out towards the water. As they both looked out at the evening sky, Noah looked nervous. He turned to Dora and took a deep breath. "Dora, you know I'll be graduating soon and will be starting a new job. It will be the beginning of a new life for me and I want you to be part of it. I love you Dora and was wondering if you would marry me?" Dora, for a moment was taken off guard, then looked back at Noah and smiled, her eyes filled with tears. "I love you too Noah. I couldn't see myself without you. Yes, of course I will marry you." They kissed. "But" she continued, "I'll accept under two conditions. First, that you come meet my parents and get their permission to marry. And second, we set a date after I graduate." Noah agreed without hesitation. They hugged. They were ecstatic!

Noah, a few years older than Dora was graduating in a month and was hired to start a new job at a local engineering firm. But a week before he was to begin his new job, war broke out between Lithuania and Poland. Without notice, Noah was drafted into the Army and sent to the front line to fight the invading Polish forces along the southern border. Dora was devastated. They had already made plans to meet each other's parents and to officially announce their engagement. Their plans would have to wait.

As the weeks went by, the war was not going well for the smaller, less equipped Lithuanian Army. Noah's letters from the Front slowed and Dora became more and more anxious. She found little comfort knowing he was not actually in combat, but assigned to a support transport unit providing medical supplies to the troops in the field. Still, she was worried about his safety. Sara and her brothers did all they could over the weeks ahead, to keep Dora positive and distracted by the news coming from the Front. Even her studies began to suffer due to her preoccupation with the war and Noah's safety.

As the news continued to filter in from the battlefield, a new semester was beginning at school. On Monday, the first day of classes, the girls were up early and were chatting away about the day ahead, when suddenly they heard a knock at the door. It was still quite early and they were both surprised to hear someone at the front door. Dora, who was still getting dressed, opened the door to see her brother Joseph standing there with a grim look on his face. He looked pale and his eyes bloodshot. Dora knew something was wrong. He began to speak. "Good Morning Sis, sorry about coming over so early, but I wanted to catch you and Sara before you headed off to school." Dora replied, "Joseph are you OK?" Joseph now stepping inside the apartment and shutting the door behind him, turned to see Sara joining her sister. "Good morning Joseph, what brings you here so early in the morning?" Dora, now anxious, was waiting for Joseph to speak. Joseph paused for a moment, gasping for air. "I'm OK, but I have some bad news. Noah's Dad called me last night to tell me that he received a telegram from Noah's commanding officer letting him know that Noah's Supply Unit was attacked by Polish troops yesterday and Noah and 3 other soldiers were severely wounded." Joseph paused for a moment, trying to catch in breath. "Noah died late last night from his wounds." Joseph continued, as tears began rolling down his face, "The commanding Officer sends his condolences. Noah"s father apologizes for not calling, but he and Mara (wife) were just too upset, so he asked me to tell both of you that he is sorry for not letting you know personally." At that moment, Dora fell to the floor and burst into tears. Sara, too stunned to say a word, ran back into the bedroom in tears and slammed the door. Both girls were devastated. Neither of the Sisters went to classes that day and the following day dropped out of school and returned home to be in the comfort of their family. They decided not to return to school for the new semester. It was a low point in Dora's life.

As the next semester began, the girls returned to Kaunas, but life for them would never be the same. Both spent most of their free time staying in their apartment studying or going to the library. It was an extremely difficult time for both of them as well as their brothers who were close friends of Noah and his family. All four children supported each other over the next few months and occasionally got together for dinner at their Sisters' apartment. They would frequently chat late into the night about Noah and how much he was part of the family. As difficult as it was to talk about Noah, conversations among the siblings were helpful towards move on with their lives.

CHAPTER 2: LIFE IN THE CAPITAL CITY

As the Sisters continued to heal from their tragic loss, David was already working as a Electrician in Kaunas on a major building project for a construction company. Having lived in a rather poor section of town when he first arrived, he now was making enough money to afford a more upscale apartment. Call it fate or coincidence, but after several weeks of searching, he found a perfect apartment in the same building as Dora and Sara. He settled in to his new residence right above them on the 4th floor.

Life was going well for David. He had a good job, was sending money home to his Mom and Sister to support the store and was enjoying living in his new surroundings. Then one day in early spring of 1938, he ran into Sara outside their apartment building. They chatted for awhile and before long they became friends. Knowing that Dora was continuing to isolate herself, Sara decided to tell Dora about a new neighbor she met who moved upstairs and was thinking about inviting him over for Sabbath dinner. Dora thought for a moment "No Sara, that's not a good idea. I'm not in the mood for company and certainly not with a man who lives in the building." Sara, sheepishly turned away to start dinner, and dropped the topic.

After several more weeks past and David and Sara got better acquainted, she again brought up the topic of inviting David over for dinner. But this time Dora was a bit more receptive to the idea, and the following Friday, Sara invited him over for Sabbath dinner. David, knew about the loss of Noah, and felt a bit awkward when he arrived on Friday night. There was little conversation between Dora and David, but Sara kept the conversation going, talking about the new movies that just came out, the economy, and a bit of gossip about a few of the residents in the building. David also added some conversation about his soccer days in high school, his Mother's shop, and his Sister who had just gotten engaged. Dinner was uncomfortable for Dora at first since she was not accustomed to male company in a social setting and still had lingering thoughts about Noah. David could feel her distance, but he did what he could to keep the conversation light and keep Dora engaged. After dinner they retired to the living room where Dora seemed a bit more comfortable. Having a glass or two of her Father's homemade Kosher wine at dinner made the evening a bit lighter, a little more relaxed. Dora began opening up a bit more to her life back home and her family, and the family farm which interested David, since he had grown up on a main street in the middle of town and didn't know much about life on a farm. It wasn't long before David's warmth and charm became evident to Dora and for the first time since Noah's death, she smiled.

As time passed, David was invited back for dinner and soon the three were making Friday Sabbath dinner a regular occurrence. On occasion, David also showed off his culinary skills which he got from his mom, by inviting the ladies to his apartment for dinner. The girls were quite impressed! The three became very close as dinners led to movies and spending more time outside the apartment. Soon Sara sensed that the Dora and David were developing a special bond, so she started coming up with excuses about why she couldn't join them on the weekends as often. So both David and Dora began going out as a couple and their bond grew even stronger. Their time together became more than friendship. They had fallen in love. Of course, Sara had that in mind right from the beginning.

Dora, knowing their relationship was serious, decided to write letters home to her parents telling them about David and how much he meant to her. She wanted the family to meet him. Unfortunately, the news about David got a rather lukewarm response from her parents since David didn't have a formal education, nor did he come from a background worthy of marrying a Rabbi's daughter. But, knowing how much David meant to Dora, the Rabbi and his wife decided to invite the couple for the Passover Seder, only a few weeks later. They were still curious to know more about the man in Dora's life.

As Passover was soon upon them, Dora, David and Sara boarded a train for Mazeikia for the Holiday and the long weekend. The girls were looking forward to spending time with family, but David was a bit nervous about meeting Dora's Father, since he didn't know how he would be received. It's not every day that a young man comes to the home of a Rabbi on Passover to ask permission to marry his daughter. Dora could tell that David was apprehensive about meeting her family, as the three boarded the train for Mazeikia. But she assured him that he would be well received and will enjoy the weekend with her family.

When the couple arrived, Dora's parents and siblings were thrilled to see them as they came through the front door. They all hugged and kissed one another, happy to know that the family was together for the first time in months. And this Passover was extra special, since Dora was bringing home a very "special guest," a man who she hoped would become her husband someday. The family all welcomed David warmly as the three walked into the house. Dora's siblings each walked over to David one by one, to introduce themselves and assured him they were happy to see him. David made sure he greeted the Rabbi and his wife in a warm but respectful manner. There were also other guests who were there for the Passover dinner. It was a tradition for Dora's father to invite a handful of people from his congregation who were alone for the Passover Holiday or couldn't afford a traditional Seder meal. This was just another reason why the Rabbi was so beloved by the entire Jewish community. He truly felt that his congregation was extended family.

Chaja and her daughters, along with Norma, spent the entire day preparing the traditional Seder dinner. Included with dinner was of course the best Kosher wine in the city which the Rabbi made himself. The Rabbi conducted the traditional Passover prayers and readings from the Old Testament, which the children as well as David took part in. During dinner the family spoke of stories from the Bible mixed with some light hearted conversation. Throughout the evening a considerable number of questions were also directed at David pertaining to his family and upbringing. A bit nervous, he replied in a respectful and thoughtful manner, hoping he was giving Dora's family the right answers.

By the end of the evening he felt quite comfortable around the table, as Dora knew he would. After dinner the Rabbi and his invited guest headed for the Rabbi's Study. The room was huge and quite intimidating as David walked over to a long leather couch, while the Rabbi sat in his oversized chair. The library's paneled walls held built in bookcases with hundreds of books, some dating back centuries. Behind the large desk there were rows of certificates and awards from the Jewish Community and other organizations. After a few minutes of silence the Rabbi with his strong deep voice asked "Well David, I hear you and Dora have become quite close over the past several months and my daughter seems very happy. She wrote Chaja and I a few letters telling us how much she loves you and that you were considering marriage, is that right?" David, feeling a bit nervous by the Rabbi's directness, looked away for a moment and then looked back at the Rabbi, "Yes, Rabbi, I love your daughter very much and we both would like to spend the rest of our lives together." "Hmmm," the Rabbi responded. "Do you feel you can support her in the job you have?" "Yes," David replied, "The construction business in Kaunas is strong and there is plenty of work for me; and my skills are still in high demand." "And what about having children, is that in your plans too?" The Rabbi asked. "Yes sir." We would like to have at least 3." "Good." The Rabbi said, in an accepting tone. "Having children is God's blessing to the world. Everyone should have children. I raised my children to think things through carefully before making a decision, especially on matters that could change their lives. I have every confidence that my daughter too will make the right decision. I have no doubt she loves you and I believe you love her too. Marriage should never be taken lightly. With love comes responsibility and commitment to each other for a lifetime. Are you prepared to offer this to her?" David replied, "Yes Sir, I would never consider asking her to marry me, unless I wanted to spend the rest of my life with her. That is a vow we made to each other." The Rabbi smiled and replied. "I see. Well then," There was a silence. The Rabbi continued, "But let's see how the rest of this weekend goes, as you get to know our family better and we get to know you." David sighed and smiled. "Yes Sir, that would be fine." They both shook hands. David and the Rabbi exited the Study and walked back into the living room where the family and other guests were chatting. They joined the conversation with the guests and family for the rest of the evening. A joyous Passover evening for all.

By the end of the weekend, Dora could see that her parents and siblings took a warm liking toward David. She knew from the outset that he would be welcomed into the family, and indeed he was. And David knew that he found a second family who was wonderful. David's Mom and Sister also met with Dora several weeks later in Kedian. They were overjoyed with the couple's decision to wed. So on June 21, 1939, the couple said "I do" in front of family and friends in a small ceremony at the Rabbi's home with the Rabbi presiding. A day the couple would remember the rest of their lives.

The following Spring Dora gave birth to their first child, a beautiful little girl, 6 pounds, 8 ounces, named Rose Miriam. It was a joyous time, but the celebration would be short lived as the winds of war were already blowing from the West and heading directly towards the couples' doorstep.

PHOTO: Downtown Kaunas, 1939
PHOTO CREDIT: Public Domain

CHAPTER 3

THE WINDS OF WAR

"The sound of marching boots could now be heard"

DATELINE – KAUNAS, LITHUANIA – 1940 -1941

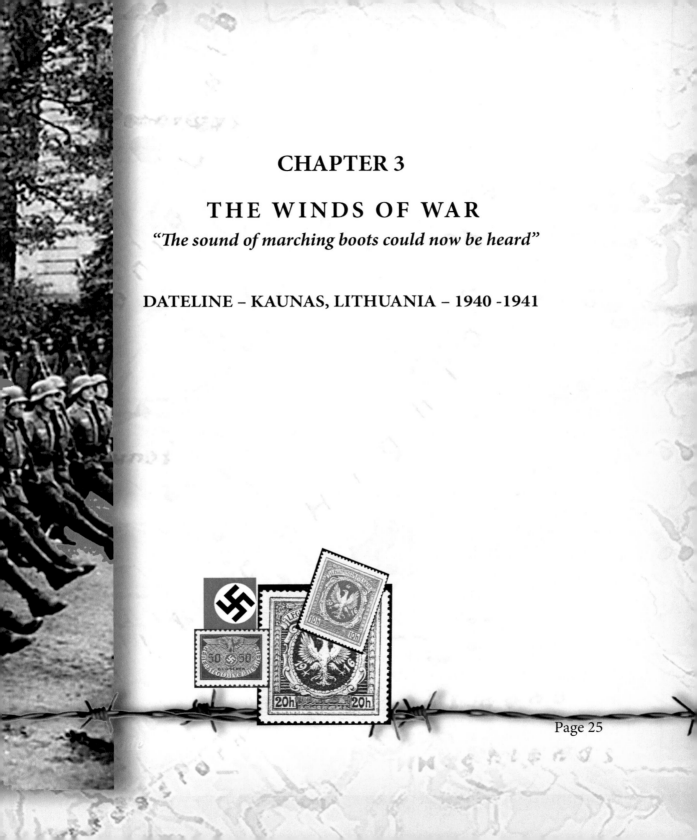

PHOTO SPREAD:
German Troops March through Warsaw

PHOTO CREDIT:
Public Domain via "Ping News"
and national archives.
1939 Jger Hugo (NARA) com.

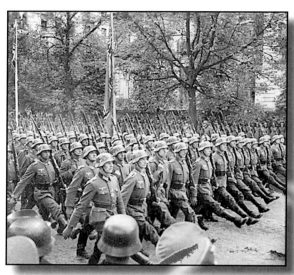

PHOTO :
German Troops advance toward Kovno.
The sign in the photograph reads:
Kaunas (Kovno) 98 Kilometers.

PHOTO CREDIT:
Lithuanian Photographic and
Video Archives. Public Domain

CHAPTER 3

THE WINDS OF WAR
"The sound of marching boots could now be heard"

DATELINE – KAUNAS, LITHUANIA – 1940 -1941

Dora and David settled into a two-bedroom flat in Kaunas with their new baby Rose. David was still working as an electrician, while Dora stayed at home taking caring of her daughter and maintaining their small but comfortable apartment. Although Dora loved being a new mother, she hoped to return to teaching someday.

Dora's sister Sara and her two older brothers now lived nearby, and Dora and David frequently invited them over to their flat for dinner. They spent many evenings reminiscing about life back home and sharing their hopes for the future. Sara, David and Joseph adored their sweet baby niece, and there was never enough time to play with her before her bedtime.

Dora and David had been staying in touch with their families by mail over the past year, and were making plans to visit them for the Holy Holidays, only a few months away. In the meantime, they tried to avoid thinking about the deteriorating conditions outside their front door. Soviet troops had taken over the government through a communist coup d'etat, setting up their own provisional puppet government in Lithuania. Political repressions followed, with mass deportations to Siberia of 130,000 Baltic citizens (both Jew and non-Jew) who were accused of being enemies of the state. This invasion of the Baltic States by the Russians was all part of the Non-Aggression Pact between Hitler and Stalin a year earlier. (1)

As news spread in Kaunas of Germany's invasion of Poland and France, Lithuanians were under Soviet oppression which took away all Lithuanian sovereignty and individual rights. As the Nazi onslaught continued through Poland, thousands of soldiers and civilians were killed, the largest group being Polish Jews. As Nazi Storm Troopers "steamrolled" over town after town, many of the Polish Jewish citizenry were rounded up and transported into concentration camps as political prisoners or enemies of the state. In the camps, thousands were put to death by mass executions, starvation or forced labor.

The Germans continued their rampage over Poland throughout 1940, which was a blatant violation of the non-aggression pact between Hitler and Stalin as well as the Treaty of Versailles which ended World War I. In response,the Soviet Union began preparing for war. Russia quickly fortified their positions with thousands of troops around Lithuania and the other Baltic countries to create a "firewall" to protect their recently acquired annex countries for the Russian Homeland. While in Germany, Hitler and his generals were boastful of their victories in the battlefield and felt confident they would succeed to "Germanize" Europe for the German people. And through all the plundering and destruction caused by the Nazis, the removal of all Jews was always one of their top objectives. For in Hitler's eyes, the Jews who were solely responsible for the loss of World War I and the humiliation of Germany; the Jews who were a direct threat to the Aryan people, the "Master Race"; the Jews who were seeking world domination. Without their total removal of Jews from the planet, there would never be peace in the world. All Nazi propaganda which fed the Nazi "war-machine" and the German people.

As the war continued to escalate, Germany's mighty and powerful "war machine" was unmatched in most of Europe, but it wouldn't be long before Germany would be faced its greatest challenge yet; capturing its greatest prize, the Soviet Union. It would be a face off between two powerful nations, and two powerful ideologies, fascism on one hand (Germany) and communism (Soviet Union) on the other. A battle that would shake the world to its core.

CHAPTER 3: THE WINDS OF WAR

DATELINE – KAUNAS, LITHUANIA– JUNE, 1941:

The Germans had blasted through Polish lines and were heading east to the Lithuanian border. With Soviet forces now firmly in place in Lithuania, their first line of defense would be to stop the Germans from entering the capital city. Soviet soldiers were entrenched around the city which include several divisions of heavily armed troops and tanks to repel Germany's battled hardened infantry which appeared to be unstoppable. Soviet tanks could be seen rumbling through the city streets heading west to meet the enemy and prevent them from entering the city. City streets were now deserted, other than heavily armed military soldiers heading west. Most residents were hunkered down in their homes and apartments, while others scurried for cover in abandoned buildings and factories.

Tensions were high in Kaunas. The Germans had crossed the Lithuanian border, heading east toward the capital city. Bombs and machine gun fire could now be heard in the distance, as additional Russian reinforcements were seen heading toward the battlefield. Loud explosions from German artillery and Soviet aircraft could be heard in the distance David and Dora were huddled with their daughter, in their apartment praying the bombardment would stop. Dora held Rose against her as she shook in fear.

As the Germans got closer, the machine gun fire and bomb explosions became deafening. The couple soon realized it was unsafe to be in their apartment. Dora held Rose as David quickly gathered up food, water and diapers for the baby. They moved swiftly to the basement of the building where they believed it was safer, since the basement had no windows and the walls were constructed with heavy reinforced concrete. As they entered the basement, they could smell the dampness in the room which was dark and dirty. The basement was filled with old furniture and odds and ends, used for storage by the tenants. The room was nevertheless three times the size of the upstairs apartments. The cement foundation and dirt floor made it a perfect shelter from the bombs and machine gunfire which could now be heard outside the basement door. As they positioned themselves away from the door, they noticed a couple with their two small children who had already staked out a claim along the back wall. They greeted each other with a nod as they were preoccupied bullets hitting the buildings in the distance.

Not long after David, Dora and Rose settled in, many more people began filing into the basement, some with children, some with dogs and cats. Someone even came in with a caged parrot. Soon the basement became so overcrowded that people had to be turned away at the door, causing tempers to flare and fights to break out. Fortunately, the owner of the building, along with a few tenants, were able to push people away and locked the door. Many of those denied entrance were not tenants. They came from surrounding buildings in the neighborhood and had nowhere to run and no place to hide. They needed shelter quickly from the raining bombs and machine gun fire that was becoming more intense by the minute. Those outside the door were banging and screaming to let them in, but it was to no avail. There was no room for even one more body. Eventually those outside moved away from the door and began running towards other buildings along the side streets. Whether they made it to safety was never known.

Many in the room knew each other; others did not. David and Dora were relieved to see their best friends, Samuel and Regina, who occupied the apartment next to theirs, huddled on the other side of the basement. Dora and David found a way to push through the crowd. "Hello Regina, so good to know that you and Sam are safe." Dora said. "Yes, good to see you and David, too," Regina replied. "I don't know what is going to happen. And who knows how long we're going to be here." Regina continued, "Things are bad, very bad. I was hoping that the Russians would stop the Germans from entering the city, but it doesn't look like that's going to happen now." Sam began to speak, "Yes, we were shocked to see how fast everything deteriorated. All Regina and I could do was to grab some food and valuables and head down here. Running toward the Russian border may have been a better way to go." David replied, "Running Sam? To the Russian border,? The Russians would just as soon kill a Jew as they would a German. No, Sam, coming here was the right thing to do."

As the thundering noise of machine guns and artillery shells continued to rain down on the city, the basement was getting hotter by the minute and the air was getting thin. They were packed like sardines, and many felt they would soon suffocate. The owner of the building decided to open the door to let some air in, but it only helped those closest to the door. Those in the back were still laboring for air. When there was a lull in the fighting, a few tenants actually went back upstairs, while others left the building altogether due to the heat and lack of oxygen. Where they went, no one knew. Those who remained were able to make it through the rest of the night, but it was a night that felt like an eternity.

The next day, the scene was grim. After less than two days of battle, there were already Soviet troops retreating through the streets of Kaunas. A steady stream of horse-drawn wagons and armed personnel carriers carrying the wounded could be seen from the building. Not far behind were converted trucks and cars, with red cross markings on the sides identifying them as ambulances, carrying more wounded. Many of the wounded, both civilian and Soviet/Lithuanian soldiers did not survive. Soviet soldiers who could walk looked dazed and oblivious to the explosions and sirens around them. Artillery guns from the invading Germans continued to bombard the city. Rose started to cry, her small voice ringing out in fear from the noise coming from the streets. Dora cradled Rose in her arms and rocked back and forth to calm them both. Small arms fire continued throughout the morning, as the retreating Soviets put up their last effort to hold the line within the city. As the bullets continued to fly, screams of people hit by flying shrapnel and bullets could be heard coming from outside the door. The fighting continued through the day, with brief interruptions as soldiers were taking up new positions around the city before resuming the fight. No one in the hot overcrowded basement slept that night, except for baby Rose.

THE VOW

DATELINE: KAUNAS - JUNE 25, 1941:

The next morning, there was a strange stillness: No sound of guns, no bombs or explosions, no tanks or trucks rolling through the streets, no screams from those who were shot or dying, just eerie silence.

In the distance, a faint sound of voices could be heard. The voices were growing louder and louder as those in the basement listened intently. As the voices became more distinguishable, those in the basement could now hear a chorus of men's voices, heavy voices, **GERMAN** voices. The voices were those of German SS soldiers, singing with mighty self-assurance and pride. They were singing a German victory song written for the German "Conquerors". Soon the boots of the marching soldiers could be heard distinctly in front of the apartment building. The German's heavy boots shook the ground which was felt inside the underground bunker. Everyone inside the basement was stricken with fear. Some of the women began to weep. The men stood stone faced and silent. The Germans had arrived.

"Could all of this be a dream?" David thought. "Could all the joy over the past few years now be crumbling around us? What would the future hold? Where would we go? How would we survive?" He and the group did not dare make a sound as they sat and waited in their darkened hiding place, uncertain to what the next moment would bring.

FOOTNOTES:

1. In 1939 Germany and Russia signed a nonaggression pact for 10 years. The proposal stipulated that neither country would aid any third party that attacked either signatory. The proposal also contained a secret protocol specifying the spheres of influence by both countries. Both Adolf Hitler and Joseph Stalin agreed that Western Poland would be invaded by Germany and annexed into Germany's sphere of influence, while Eastern Poland and the Baltic Region of Estonia, Latvia and Lithuania would be occupied by Russia, each country grabbing huge land masses to be annexed into their respective countries.

(Molotov-Ribbontrop Pact-Wikipedia)

PHOTO:
Adolf Hitler Making presentation in Germany 1933

PHOTO CREDIT:

PHOTO:
Portrait of Adolf Hitler

PHOTO CREDIT:
This file is licensed under the Creative Commons Attribution-Share Alike 3.0 Germany (https://creativecommons.org licenses/by-sa/3.0/de/deed.en) license. Attribution: Bundesarchiv, Bild 183-H1216-0500-002/CC-BY-SA 3.0

PHOTO:
Joseph Stalin (Russia) and J. Von Rippentrop (Germany) signing a non-aggression Pact in 1939

PHOTO CREDIT:
Wikipedia Commons
In the Common Domain.

CHAPTER 4
KAUNAS FALLS

*"When we are no longer able to change a situation,
we are challenged to change ourselves."*

Viktor Frankl

DATELINE:
KAUNAS LITHUANIA – JUNE 1941

PHOTO SPREAD:
Russian Tanks roll through the streets of Kaunas during Soviet occupation. 1941

PHOTO CREDIT:
United States Holocaust Museum courtesy of photographer George Birman. Photo No 123036

CHAPTER 4
KAUNAS FALLS

*"When we are no longer able to change a situation,
we are challenged to change ourselves."*

Viktor Frankl

DATELINE: KAUNAS LITHUANIA – JUNE 1941

The following morning, the building's residents remained in the basement, with only a few brave souls ascending to the upper floors to rummage through their apartments for provisions and supplies that would sustain them in the basement below. For how long they would need to stay in the basement, no one knew. For the brave Souls returning to the upper floors, their lives were at risk, as stray bullets and machine gun fire could still be heard hitting the rooftops and nearby buildings.

As the Germans surveyed the town over next few days, there was news on the street that many Jews, men, women and children were being attacked and killed in their homes by local anti-Semitic Lithuanian mobs who sided with the Germans. Many non-Jewish Lithuanians viewed the Nazis as liberators from the harsh Soviet rule over the past year due to the non-aggression pact between Germany and the Soviet Union. (1) The Lithuanians now hoped they could reestablish their independence, or at least autonomy, by killing Jews in order to please the conquering "overlords", the Germans. But there was another reason why the Lithuanians wanted to spill Jewish blood: Many Lithuanians were known to be anti-Semitic going back centuries. Some looked upon the Jews as different from the rest of the population, believing they were pro-Soviet and not supporting Lithuanian sovereignty. The mobs on the street especially asserted that the Lithuanian Jews had collaborated with the Soviets, which caused for the annexation of their country in 1940. An assertion which was never substantiated.

Within days of German occupation, people slowly began to leave their shelters and survey the aftermath of war. They saw burnt-out buildings, charred army vehicles smoldering wagons, and dead bodies everywhere. The Nazis, now in control of Lithuania, made it clear to the local government that it was their responsibility to force the local citizenry to dispose of the dead however they wished. It was a horror that no resident wanted to face.

As the Nazi field generals arrived in Kaunas to begin establishing government rule over the region, their first order was to arrange a series of agitation rallies with the local non-Jewish Lithuanian population to instigate further action against the Jews. Although Lithuanian officials at first refused to participate in the slaughter, the Germans found an ally in a Lithuanian paramilitary group of about 600 men, who converged on the city and its working class suburb of Slobodka (Jewish Quarter), who began killing Jews anywhere they can find them. The German generals had no problem handing off the mass killing of Jews to the Lithuanians, rather than leaving it to the German soldiers, for it was bad PR. The Nazis just wanted as many Jews eliminated as possible, regardless to who did the killing.

With the "green light" to proceed, the Lithuanians arrested hundreds of Jews and political prisoners for immediate execution throughout the city, while another group of Lithuanian Nazis began a killing spree within the Jewish Quarter. By the conclusion of this killing spree, 3,800 Jews were slaughtered, including Dora's two brothers David and Joseph. Concurrently, an additional 1,200 Jews were murdered in surrounding towns and villages, including David's mother and sister. Further north in Mazeikiai, Dora's remaining family was murdered by Nazi SS and Lithuanian pro-Nazi mobs, except for her younger sister Riva, who moved to Finland a year earlier. In Kaunas, the word spread that a hospital was raided, and Jewish patients had been poisoned, while in another sector of town closest to the Jewish Quarter, a city block was sealed off and an infirmary was burned to the ground, where most of the patients and medical staff had perished. Most of the synagogues in the city were also destroyed.

A few days after the mass killings, the German Authorities announced that for the protection of the Jewish residents in Kaunas, the German government would be creating a "safe zone" inside the city's Jewish Quarter. All Jews were ordered to make preparations to move to this area for their own protection by August 15, 1941, only a month away. This "safe zone" was called the Kovno Ghetto, (Kovno Russian translation for Kaunas). As the announcement was made by the Nazi hierarchy within Kaunas, a number of edicts were issued. Among them were:

1. *Jews who fled Kaunas at the beginning of the occupation had no rights to return to their apartments. Returning Jews would be shot, and those harboring Jews would be arrested.*

2. *ALL Jews were ordered to wear the Yellow Star of David on both the front and back of the left side of their garments. Jews without the markings would be shot on the spot. (The Nazis and their collaborators used paper records and local information to identify Jews to be apprehended or killed.)*

3. *Jews were not allowed to walk on any sidewalk and only permitted to walk in the gutter.*

4. *Jews were not allowed to sell any property.*

5. Jews would not be allowed to go outside of the Ghetto unless is was related to work as assigned by the German Military.

6. Jews were not permitted to use any public transportation or to enter any public establishment.

7. Jews were not permitted to have radios, and were ordered to turn all radios in at a designated drop-off locations within the Ghetto.

Once the edicts were issued, the German commanding officer and his generals decided that the Jews were to select among themselves a group of prominent members of the community to act as a council, through which all orders by the Nazi military would be issued. Among the functions of the newly formed council would be to represent the populous within the Ghetto. And most importantly, the Nazi Commandant made clear there would be no more "excesses", (i.e. killings, against Jews once all edicts were followed). The news about the creation of the Ghetto spread quickly among the Jewish residents of the city. Particularly reassuring was the news that there would be no more excesses towards the Jewish population.

Within a few days, more Jewish residents came out of their homes to get necessities and other services. German assurances were given that there would be no more killing if orders were followed. By mid-July, the boundaries of the ghetto were clearly defined and orders were given to the Jews to start looking for apartments inside the Jewish Quarter.

A mad scramble ensued to secure living quarters for thousands of Jews. Jews with money offered their luxury apartments in exchange for small apartments inside the new Ghetto boundaries on the south side of town. A bidding war began over who could pay more to rent an apartment inside the Ghetto from Lithuanian residents. Those Jews who had no money were left to fend for themselves. The Lithuanians had a choice of over eight thousand apartment units outside the Ghetto to move into, while the Jews had to move thirty thousand people into approximately one thousand units inside the Ghetto. Most of the apartments were half the size of the apartments the Jews had to vacate. The scramble for space was furious for both Jews and non-Jews. Luckily, David and Dora found a small apartment near the river, through David's work friend from the construction site. It was difficult for David and Dora to leave so much of their furniture behind because there was no space in their smaller apartment. Many of the pieces had been given to them as wedding presents. Nevertheless, they were grateful to be alive and hopefully safe within the confines of the newly established Ghetto.

PHOTO: German solders with Reindeer February 1941 in Karasjok

PHOTO CREDIT: Licensed under the Creative Commons Attribution-Share alike 2.0 Generic license.

FOOTNOTES:

(1)churches and synagogues were closed. All merchants, including Jews, lost their stores, and those who owned factories had them confiscated also.

Although some Jews supported a version of socialism or communism, the majority did not. Nevertheless, this did not prevent Lithuanian nationalists and others from claiming that Jews as a whole were collaborating with the Soviet occupiers. Many of the "Locals" argued that Jews controlled Lithuania and the Soviet Union, and were conspiring to take over the world.

(United States Holocaust Museum, Kovno, Holocaust Encyclopedia.)

(2)The Nazis and their collaborators used paper records and local information to identify Jews to be apprehended or killed. Records included those created by Jewish communities of their members, parish records of Protestant and Catholic churches (for converted Jews), government tax records, and police records, including registries of Jews compiled by local, collaborating police.

In Nazi occupied countries including the Baltic countries, Nazi officials required Jews to identify themselves as Jewish, and many complied, fearing the consequences if they did not. In many Nazi occupied countries including Lithuania, local citizens often showed authorities where their Jewish neighbors lived, if they did not themselves help in rounding them up. Jews in hiding lived in constant fear of being identified and denounced to German officials by Lithuanians in exchange for monetary or other rewards. It should be noted that the location and identification of Nazi victims did not rely on modern technology, as sometimes claimed in the popular media. Nevertheless, It is true that punch card machines produced by Hollerith Machine, a subsidiary of the American com-

pany IBM (International Business Machines), were used in Nazi Germany, as in the United States and many western European countries in the 1920s and 1930s, for processing and sorting information on households that had been gathered by census workers going door to door. Aggregated census data processed by Hollerith machines could provide the Nazi government with information on how many Jews lived in a particular German city, since the census of 1939 included data on "race," identifying who was a Jew as defined by the Nuremberg Laws.

Technology even for such limited purposes as census tabulations, however, would not have been found in economically less developed German-occupied eastern Europe, such as Lithuania, and the other Baltic countries as well as the Soviet Union, where the vast majority of Jews lived. About 75%, or 4.5 million of the 6 million Jews killed in the Holocaust, lived within that region.

Nevertheless, the Hollerith machine technology was introduced throughout the concentration camp system in 1942, not to locate and identify people to be killed but as a way of managing and tracking data on living prisoners. This was particularly true with regard to their professional and occupational skills, some of which the Germans needed to support their war production.

(Wikipedia-IBM and World War II)

CHAPTER 5
INSIDE THE KOVNO GHETTO

"Who Lives, Who Dies"

DATELINE: LITHUANIA - JULY, 1941

PHOTO SPREAD:
WHO LIVES...WHO DIES

PHOTO CREDIT:
Auschwitz Album, Public
Domain, courtesy of Yad Vashem
Holocaust Remembrance Center,
Jerusalem, Israel

PHOTO: Inspection of troops during Warsaw Ghetto Uprising.

PHOTO CREDIT:
Wikipedia Commons: unknown author, Stroop Connection, Common
License.

CHAPTER 5
INSIDE THE KOVNO GHETTO

"Who Lives, Who Dies"

DATELINE: LITHUANIA - JULY, 1941

During the moving period which started in mid-July 1941, the city was in total disarray. The moving process was exhausting. With thirty thousand Jews on the move, vehicles were at a premium, so David hired two burly Lithuanians with a horse-drawn wagon to move their belongings to the other side of town. The prices the Jews were being charged for moving 4 miles was outrageous, but David and Dora had no choice. Not paying the price Lithuanians asked would have meant moving into the Ghetto practically empty handed. Even so, they took very few personal items, as they knew space in their smaller apartment would be limited. With only the essentials, and a few pieces of living room furniture, given as wedding presents, the men quickly loaded up their horse-drawn wagon to began their move across town. Having very little space on the wagon the couple and their child were crammed into the back seat which made the ride very uncomfortable, especially with the oppressive July heat and humidity. As they began to pull away from the apartment Dora's eyes began to fill with tears as she thought they would never return to the neighborhood which held such special meaning. The apartment was in a great location and it was the couples first home together. They also developed close friendships with the neighbors in the building and now it would all be a memory. "I'm really going to miss the apartment, David. It really felt like home. Leaving is still so hard to accept. Why does there have to be a war and why are so many people dying?" David just looked straight ahead without saying a word, only glancing at his daughter wishing the driver would get going. As the wagon began to pull away, Dora looked back one last time at their apartment building and suddenly gasped. There in the distance she saw her best (non-Jewish) girlfriend, Francine, coming out of their apartment building wearing one of her favorite spring jackets, which she accidentally left in the apartment. The jacket was given to her by David when they first married. "What's wrong?" David called out. "Why are you crying?" Dora pointed back to the apartment building, "Look!", her voice now cracking. David could see Francine walking down the street wearing Dora's jacket. Dora was heartbroken, knowing Francine was one of her best friends.

As they continued down the road to the Ghetto, the wagon suddenly came to a halt. The traffic going into the Ghetto had become totally backed up with cars, trucks, and people walking on foot. The ride took much longer than had been expected, and the heat and humidity was oppressive. When they finally arrived in the Jewish Quarter, they felt they were not in the same city. The neighborhood was totally run down, the paved streets were now dirt roads, the buildings were not well maintained and the smell of garbage permeated the hot July air. As they climbed down from the wagon, they looked up to see a three story old wooden building that hadn't been maintained in years. The stairs leading up to their first floor apartment was made from plywood and could hardly withstand the weight of anyone climbing the stairs. They also noticed there were very few curtains on the windows of the building and the hallways were dark. When they entered their first floor apartment, David looked around and sighed, "This certainly doesn't feel like home. But, I guess for now this will have to do." The two large men quickly unloaded the wagon and threw their belongings inside the hallway leading to their apartment. "Pay up Mr." The Driver shouted. "Due to the traffic our fee has gone up by fifty dollars". "What?" David asked. "That's right, Mister, fifty bucks, five, zero," as the Driver smirked showing only two front teeth. David was furious and raised his voice, "But that wasn't our fault Mister, We had no way of knowing that the traffic was going to be this bad!" The Driver, angrily replied, "Listen friend, you don't pay up we'll load the furniture back on the truck and leave!" David knew he was backed into a corner and had no choice. He reached in his pocket and paid the men, begrudgingly. After the men left, David turned to Dora and said, "I was angered more about how those two guys treated us than the fee. It's people like them that make me wonder if we'll be safe here."

Surprisingly, the couple managed to fit all their belongings into their small living space, but barely. The crib fit fine against their bed, but the small love seat and dresser left little room for anything else. Dora, relieved to have unpacked, sighed, "Well, it's small but its home and we're all together. That's all that matters." She picked up Rose from the floor and placed her in the crib for her afternoon nap. David walked over and gave Dora a hug. "We'll be fine, my beautiful wife, just fine." Little did they know that within a few hours, there would be two more families coming through the door to call their apartment home.

As the days passed, there were new edicts being established almost every day against the Jews. The latest being;

1. *All main streets in town were off-limits to Jews and they can only use side streets between six am to eight pm.*

2. *No Jew was permitted to have cameras, typewriters, or bicycles and they were instructed to turn over all such items to the local authorities by August 15th.*

3. *Jews who were not in the Ghetto by August 15th would be arrested and shot immediately.*

4. *Jews were not allowed to employ non-Jews for help including domestic help.*

5. *Jews were forbidden to go to market to shop for food. Food would be distributed to them by German soldiers or designated Lithuanian representatives.*

On August 15th, 1941 the ghetto was sealed, confining 30,000 Jews where only 6,000 residents had lived previously. Barbed wire fences were erected around the Ghetto, with only one gate to enter and leave. The entrance was closely monitored by heavily armed SS Soldiers along with aggressive German Shepard guard dogs. In addition, the entire perimeter was heavily patrolled 24/7 by SS soldiers to make sure no one escaped by attempting to breach the barb wired fences.

The flat David and Dora occupied was located near the river and the main gate of the compound that faced the woods. There was also an abandoned synagogue across the street, which was converted into offices used by the Jewish Council, responsible for maintaining order inside the Ghetto. Their apartment, which previously housed one couple and a child, was now the home for 6 adults and 5 children.

DAILY LIFE IN THE GHETTO:

Within two weeks after arriving in the Ghetto, brutal house searches began. Under the command of high-ranking SS Officers, soldiers were directed to raid apartments through-out the ghetto confiscating anything of value such as gold, silver, furniture, clothing and electrical appliances. Anything of value was loaded onto trucks outside the buildings and taken away to be distributed to military officials. The Germans searched through drawers, closets, shelves, nothing was left untouched. Any resistance or complaints from residents was met with severe beatings. Gold and Silver jewelry were of particular interest. Wedding bands and engagement rings were taken off the hands of many residents, including Dora and David, which was devastating for the couple. In addition, a few of David's best suits and shoes were also confiscated along with several of Dora's dresses.

Such unannounced searches continued over many months, with the Germans hoping they would find more valuables with each subsequent raid. In some instances, residents were beaten or even shot in their apartments for no apparent reason other than the Nazis wanted to send "a message" to the rest of the residents in the apartment buildings.

By October, there was a major edict carried out by the German Military requiring healthy men, women, and children into forced labor brigades to work outside the Ghetto. Projects included heavy manual labor construction on highways and roads, renovating building for the military and digging anti-tank ditches on the outskirts of town to impede any enemy from advancing towards the city. Inside the Ghetto, the Jewish Council established workshops for those who could not participate in the Labor Brigades, because of health reasons, or age. Such workshops employed hundreds of Jews inside the ghetto to produce small handcrafted products for military or civilian use. The Council hoped the workshops would spare the lives of Jews who were too old, too sick, or too young to work outside the gates. The council believed as long as the residents were productive they would be kept alive to support the German military. Many residents survived, at least temporarily through these workshops.

Inside the Ghetto, food was distributed sporadically, usually every week, with residents receiving a few slices of bread, 100 grams of horse meat, and, occasionally, one small potato. With rations being so minuscule, some of the frail and elderly as well as the very young could not sustain themselves and died. With food rations being so limited, a black market arose to buy or barter for food and essential items for daily living by the ghetto inhabitants. The market flourished, as provisions were smuggled into the Ghetto by Jewish laborers who worked outside fences or people who bartered through the fence. To obtain items such as vegetables, fruit, butter and sugar, the Jews had to barter personal belongings, such as shoes, watches, jewelry pieces, clothing and other valuables. For many, bartering made the difference between life and starving to death. Yet bartering was dangerous. If a Jew and a non-Jew were caught in the act of exchanging goods or services, both were immediately shot by SS guards. For the Jews, bartering was even more treacherous, for they did not always know who they were approaching at the fences. Were they interacting with trustworthy people or fervent anti-Semitics who would turn them in to authorities at the drop of a hat. Undercover Gestapo agents dressed as ordinary citizens were everywhere, which made bartering even more dangerous. Jews were risking their lives everyday for nothing more than a slice of bread, an apple or a stick of butter to survive.

Inside the Ghetto, the most terrifying experience was the so-called **"Selections"** conducted regularly without notice by German SS Officers. When **"Selections"** occurred, designated German SS officers would conduct raids and forcibly removed people from their apartments and grabbed people off the streets, forcing them into the city square. These actions took place anytime, day or night. The number of people brought into the square for Selection could range from several hundred to nearly a thousand residents, taking hours to complete. The numbers depended on weekly quotas needed for work details and for extermination to reduce overall Jewish population. The numbers "selected" had to stand at attention for hours until the selection process was completed. Those who couldn't stand for the duration of the selection process were taken away and beaten or shot. Residents in poor health or too old were also eliminated, for they were no use to the Germans.

Further, residents who were found hiding to avoid Selection were also taken away and executed. Once assembled, the Jews were ordered to form two lines. One line for women and children under the age of 16 and the other for men. At the front of both lines stood several SS Officers. As the Captives came forth one by one to face the Guards, they were asked their trade or profession and were physically examined to see if they were fit for work. If the lead officer found individuals healthy enough to work, he pointed them to the right; those judged unfit to work for whatever reason were pointed to the left and later transported in the 9th fort for execution. (1) The experience of going through this selection process on an ongoing basis was terrifying, and prompted many to commit suicide before the process even began. Many also tried to escape before they were taken for "Selection", but were shot before they reached the fences.

It was not long after the Ghetto was sealed that there was an announced **"Selection"** raid on their apartment building that David, Dora and Sara lived. All were taken to the city square where two lines formed. Men and boys formed one line, women and girls formed the other. Everyone in line knew that their lives hung in the balance, based upon the decision by the attending Officer. As they moved through the line one by one in an orderly but slow manner, the fear was palatable. They knew they were just moments away from facing the jury, judge and executioner, in a Nazi uniform. A Nazi soldier, who just months earlier, could have been working as a car mechanic, or a sheep herder on a farm in Bavaria. As the Officer called "next." Dora and her sister slowly stepped closer to the front of the line for questioning and examination. Only moments away from Dora being called for examination, she turned to Sara, and whispered "pinch your cheeks." Sara, totally puzzled by what Dora was saying, whispered back, "What?" she asked "What do you mean?" Dora taking her fingers, pinched her own cheeks, and again whispered, "pinch your cheeks, Sara, like this, (showing Sara what she needed to do). You have to get some color in your face, so you look healthy." Sara pinched her cheeks, as she was told. Dora nodded her head in approval.

Dora was next in line. She was barely able to stand, as she felt like she was going to faint. The Officer's voice suddenly rang out **"NEXT, NEXT IN LINE, STEP UP!"** Dora, moved closer to the officer to stand in front of a tall, muscular man in his 30s in full uniform who smelled of alcohol. "What is your profession Jewess?" the Officer blared out. Dora, almost unable to breathe pushed the words out the word, "Teacher". **"YOU CALL ME SIR, BITCH",** the Officer yelled out. "Teacher, Sir" Dora replied. "What kind of teacher?" the guard asked, "Do you mean a teacher who teaches Pigs how to clean toilets or how to have babies?" Dora, now shaking, hesitated, then replied in a submissive tone, "I teach children, elementary school, mostly reading and writing." "Do you have any children?" the Officer asked. "One Sir" she replied. "OK, turn around and let me look at you." The Officer got out of his chair and examined her arms and shoulders. "Show me your hands, or I will cut them off," the soldier barked. Dora extended her arms to show the officer her hands that were cut and bruised from work detail. He looked at her face. Dora did not look back at him.

"Look at me Jewess" he shouted. **"I SAID LOOK AT ME, PIG TEACHER!"** She looked reluctantly, trying not to connect directly into his eyes, while holding back her tears. There was silence, as the officer continued to stare at her. Suddenly he yelled out "Ok, to the right, go!!!" .... **"NEXT".** David, Dora and Sara experienced a number of such "Selections" for the duration of their time in the Ghetto. Each time barely escaping the "hang man's noose". Truly nothing short of a miracle!

While in the Ghetto, David performed several jobs for the Nazis, although mostly of his labor was outside the gates. Working outside the Ghetto was torture, as workers were faced with harsh conditions, working in the bitter cold or the oppressive heat, 12-16 hours a day, 6 days a week. The Laborers were organized into work details dressed in tattered clothes and footwear (if they were lucky). They marched in formation for long distances, many already exhausted from the constant long hours of work over weeks at a time. Many collapsed and died as they marched, even before they reached their work destination.

The work outside the gates varied, based on German needs to support the military command. From working at construction sites and munition factories to digging anti-tank ditches along roadways and performing other labor-intensive work on roads or factories. The most desired jobs for the workers were those which had contact with the local population, which was forbidden by the Germans. Such contact gave the prisoners an opportunity to exchange valuables for food, despite the danger of being caught and shot by the Nazi guards. In addition to the opportunity to exchange items for food, those who worked outside the fences were generally safe from execution, since most "Selections" occurred during daytime hours inside the Ghetto.

While inside the ghetto, Dora and Sara worked mostly in the cleaning detail. They were responsible for cleaning the Officers' housing units. Their days started very early, around 5 am. They were responsible for cleaning and scrubbing the barracks, including the kitchen and latrine using just a scrub brush and soapy water. If the Head Officer believed areas were not clean enough, Dora and Sara would be ordered to start the entire process over again. Sometimes two and three times in the same day.

One morning in January of 1942, prior to going to work, David was selected with 49 other men for summary execution for no apparent reason, but he was pulled from the group by a Gestapo Official just in time. The Official knew that David was an electrician and his skills would be of value to the Germans, both inside and outside the ghetto. He was given a reprieve, but he nevertheless had to stand there and watch the shootings of 50 Jews, many his friends. An event that haunted him throughout his life.

CONCERTS IN THE GHETTOS:

As a respite from the fear, death and destruction faced daily by the Ghetto residents, the Germans occasionally permitted Sunday afternoon classical music concerts, performed by accomplished Jewish musicians at the fire station across from the city square.

Listening to beautiful music played by accomplished Jewish musicians for an hour or so provided an escape for both David and Dora, as well as many of the residence who didn't know if the next day they would be alive. The orchestra provided dozens of concerts for many in the Ghetto especially during the Spring and Summer months. Sometimes, after the concerts concluded, some of the audience would look up at the night sky and gaze at the stars. Some began to weep, as the music and the night sky reminded them of how life used to be before the war began. The evening ended when they slowly headed back to their overcrowded apartments and their reality and cried again.

BUILDING A HIDING PLACE:

Some Ghetto residents realized it was essential to build hiding places in their apartment to escape from unannounced raids on the apartment buildings. Or worse yet, to be rounded up for **"selection"**. It was important to build a hiding place in total secrecy, which they did

together in the middle of the night for weeks. They dug a deep square hole under a floorboard in their small room. They removed the dirt through a window which faced the woods, when guards were not patrolling the fences. They equipped the deep hole with electricity, and supplies which David bartered for on the black market or stole from his worksite. They stored enough food for at least a week, buying non-perishables from non-Jews outside the fence, as well as saved rations that were distributed by the Germans. Sliding the love seat and a small carpet over the hole underneath the floorboard made a perfect hiding place which was nearly impossible to detect during numerous raids by German guards in the months ahead.

FOOTNOTES:

At the time Lithuania was part of the Russian Empire) surrounded the city of Kaunas. During (1) A chain of nine military fortifications constructed in the nineteenth century by Russia (at German occupation, several of these forts were converted into mass extermination centers where thousands of Jews inside and outside of the Kovno were murdered. Fort IX in particular, became a major site of the killing actions inside Kovno. An estimated 40,000 people were shot to death in Fort IX between the fall of 1941 and the spring of 1944. In September 1943, the Germans began operation to exhume and burn thousands of corpses buried in Fort IX. This effort was part of a larger program undertaken by the German security police and SS Soldiers to wipe out the evidence of Nazi mass murder throughout eastern Europe.

The final large-scale killing action at the fort took place in May 1944, only two months before the liberation of the city, when a deportation transport of Jews from France was routed to Kovno for extermination.

(9th fort massacres of November, 1941, Wikipedia)

PHOTO: Opposite Page
Entering Captured City, Warsaw Ghetto Uprising, Poland.

PHOTO CREDIT:
Wikimedia: Stroop Report Common License.

CHAPTER 6
THE DEATH OF INNOCENCE...

"For the survivor who chooses to testify, it is clear: his duty is to bear

witness for the dead and for the living ...

To forget the dead would be akin to killing them

a second time."

- Elie Wiesel

DATELINE: GERMANY –

1943 - 1944

KAUNAS, LITHUANIA

PHOTO SPREAD:
Abraham Rosenthal, age 5
Emanuel age 2.
Deceased,1944 Kovno, Lithuania
(Kinder Aktion).

PHOTO CREDIT:
Yad Vasdhem,
The World Holocaust Remembrance
Center, Jerusalem, Israel

PHOTO:
Lena Shateryte was born in Kaunas,
Lithuania, in 1940. She was one of 1600 children
taken along with Rose, on March 27-28.
1944 during Kinder Aktoin
(Raid against the Children)
Deceased: 1944

PHOTO CREDIT:
Yad Vasdhem,
The World Holocaust Remembrance
Center, Jerusalem, Israel

PHOTO:
Pictured are Henia Wisgardisky (right), and her cousin, Bluma Berk. This photograph was taken a few months before Henia's mother smuggled the two girls out of the ghetto.

Both children were hidden by Lithuanian familes and survived the war.

PHOTO CREDIT:
United States Holocaust Memorial
Museum Provenance:
Henia Wisgardisky Lewin.
Source Record ID: Collections: 2006.144

PHOTO:
A young boy carrying a bowl of soup, holding food ration tickets. A five-year-old boy receives hot soup for the family from the ghetto soup kitchen. His father was murdered in the beginning of the war and the mother had to take care of the smaller children. They boy became the provider of the family. He was shot trying to escape from the Germans during the "Children's Action" on March 27, 1944, Kovno, Lithuania.

PHOTO CREDIT:
United States Holocaust Memorial Museum, courtesy of George Kadish Zvi Kadushin.

CHAPTER 6
THE DEATH OF INNOCENCE...

"For the survivor who chooses to testify, it is clear: his duty is to bear witness for the dead and for the living ...
To forget the dead would be akin to killing them a second time."

- Elie Wiesel

DATELINE: KAUNAS - LITHUANIA
1943-1944

By the spring of 1942, the Germans had captured vast expanses of territory, including Ukraine, Belarus, and major cities within the Soviet territory. Hundreds of thousands died on both sides, including a vast number of civilians who were targets of German aggression, especially Jewish civilians.

Hitler believed the war was going well, expecting to take both Stalingrad and Moscow within months, not years. To achieve victory, Germany stabilized a front from Leningrad to the south, with their target being the oil fields so vitally needed to overtake the entire country and expand Germany's dominance. But in 1943, Stalin mounted a counterattack and won back many Soviet cities that had been taken by Hitler over the past two years. The tables had finally turned for the Soviets, as Germany was retreating, and Stalingrad and the oil fields remained in Soviet hands. This came at a great cost, as over 800,000 people lost their lives during the fighting. The battle for Stalingrad was one of the Bloodiest battles of World War II.

In early spring of 1944, the Russians were advancing quickly to retake the Baltic countries of Lithuania, Estonia, and Latvia. As a result, a directive came down from German High Command in Berlin to close down and liquidate the remaining Jewish ghettos in eastern Europe, including the Kovno Ghetto. The Germans wanted to leave no trace of the unimaginable atrocities committed since the Nazis came to power. Those still alive in the Ghettos were ordered to be executed or sent east to Germany for resettlement to other concentration camps. Even during the final years of the war, the Nazis still found Jewish slave labor valuable towards the war effort and just as importantly, an efficient way to reduce the Jewish population by working the Jews to death or by execution.

In Berlin, there were still some in Hitler's inner circle who argued that the remaining Jews were needed as workers to continue producing armaments to push back the Allied Offensive, while others believed keeping the Jews alive would benefit Germany as they could be used as a "bargaining chip" to negotiate a truce with the Allied Forces. Hitler, on the other hand, was adamant that ALL Jews were enemies of the state and must be done away with once and for all. There was no place for any Jew who could not work, including children.

Since the beginning of the war, Jewish newborns and young children had been viewed by most Nazis as a hindrance, because they removed many women from the labor force who were vitally needed to support Germany's war effort. During the Ghettoization of the Jews in Europe, pregnant women and mothers were being constantly threatened by the Nazis with confiscation of their children. Fearing the threats, many parents responded by smuggling their babies and young children out of the Ghetto to live with non-Jewish families throughout the city. They believed their children would be safer with families outside the ghetto and that they would be returned once the war was over. Tragically, many parents never saw their children again, either because the parents were subsequently executed or because the surrogate families believed the children were now theirs. In some instances, children wanted to remain with their surrogates rather than go back to their biological families when the war ended.

On March 27th, 1944, the day seemed like any other day in the Ghetto. As usual, Dora woke beside her daughter's bed and glanced over to make sure she was still asleep. David had left for work at the aircraft factory hours earlier. As Dora turned to lie back down for a few more minutes before starting her day, she noticed a note on David's pillow which read, "Be careful my Love, more guards outside the gates this morning. Stay inside and keep Rose close. Love you." Dora jumped from her bed, feeling the chill of the morning air as she went to the window. As Dora drew back the curtains, she saw SS guards outside the gates, with leashed German Shepherd dogs at their side. Dora knew this was not a good sign. Maybe another Selection was coming. She continued to watch for several more minutes, as the number of soldiers continued to congregate. Many now inside the gates within the city square. She pondered what she would do in case another "Raid" would happen.

Another hour passed as Dora watched more and more soldiers standing along the fences across from their apartment building. Rose, by this time, was awake and was finishing her breakfast. She began to play with her new doll that her father had given her the night before, which he had made from odds and ends he found in the factory. It was now past 10 a.m., and others in the apartment were just finishing breakfast, while talking about what was happening outside the building. Everyone felt tense. It was eerily quiet for a Monday morning. Few people were on the street as most stayed inside out of fear from the soldiers gathering in the square. Suddenly a voice from loudspeakers cut through the silence.

"ATTENTION! ATTENTION! TO ALL GHETTO RESIDENTS, YOU ARE TO STAY IN YOUR APARTMENTS AND REMAIN THERE UNTIL FURTHER NOTICE. ANYONE FOUND IN THE STREET WILL BE SHOT. THERE WILL BE NO SECOND WARNING."

The warnings were repeated again and again in German, Yiddish, and Russian from loudspeakers mounted on army vehicles which slowly drove throughout the complex. Everyone inside the apartment buildings now could see additional soldiers at attention along with plain clothed Gestapo agents inside the city square. Residents began to panic running around their apartments hiding their few valuables that still were not confiscated by the Nazis in previous raids. Dora too sensed the raid was imminent. She quickly took Rose by the hand "Come Sweetheart, take Mommy's hand, we're going to play hide and seek, but you have to be very quiet." "Can I take Emily (her doll) with me. Mommy?" Rose asked. Dora smiled and replied, "Of course you can." Dora turned and slid the small table and rug away from the spot which covered the "spider hole" that she and David had built months ago. The two quickly descended below the floor into their makeshift bunker. Dora wished that David was with her, for she didn't know what she would do if she had to remain underground for any extended period of time, as her rations were limited. But she composed herself and focused on the moment, as she slid part of the rug back over the small door on the floor.

As the warnings from the loudspeakers continued to blare, the two sat quietly inside the hole. Then suddenly the warnings stopped and were replaced by loud German marching music. Heavy footsteps were suddenly heard from the street, as Nazi soldiers and Gestapo were now barging through the front door of the buildings, shouting,

"STAY INSIDE YOUR APARTMENTS! DO NOT MOVE!"

Some of the residents cried out in fear while others ran in the hallway for the front door, and were shot. The terror-stricken screams of the residents were now constant. As the heavy boot steps of the soldiers could be heard running up and down the stairs, Dora placed her hands around Rose's ears to shut out the noise. Dora quickly tried to console her, "Everything is fine Sweetheart. They are only trying to make us come out of our hiding place, but we won't let them, will we?" Dora held her daughter tightly. "This will be over soon, my darling," Rose snuggled into her mother's chest and for the moment felt safe.

With German-shepherd dogs along side the soldiers, they ransacked each apartment using hammers, axes, and crowbars to pry open any locked doors, closets, crawl spaces or suspicious walls that could be used for hiding. They were searching not for the adults but the **CHILDREN.**

Amidst the loud screams and yelling of the families inside the apartments, SS soldiers began grabbing the children and young toddlers. Quickly they carried their victims through the hallway and out the front door to awaiting trucks, as family members pursued. Their desperate chase was abruptly stopped when a few of the soldiers turned and began shooting their rifles into the ground in front of the grieving families. All they could do was watch as the trucks drove away with their crying children on-board, never to be seen again.

As the commotion from the upper floor continued, some of the soldiers turned to the sick and elderly as part of the raid. A few residents tried to jump from the windows, but were quickly captured while others were shot as they tried to run. And through this entire ordeal, Dora was frozen in fear holding her daughter under the floor, praying for the nightmare to end.

As the chaos on the upper floors began to subside, Dora sensed that the raid was over. Could God have listened to her prayers? Was this a miracle? Had they escaped the horror going on all around them? They remained under the floor for the next few hours, Dora prayed that the soldiers filled their quotas, and were not coming back. For the first time since the ordeal began, Dora breathed a sigh of relief. The loud marching music blaring from the loudspeakers which hid the screams of the children and families ended; no more soldiers were running up and down the stair; and no gunshots were heard. Only the wailing voices and screams of the families in the hallway and apartments above her were echoing through the building.

As the afternoon passed, Dora started to make her way up through the hole with Rose, when suddenly she heard the front door of their apartment building open. She quickly went back down into the hole with Rose. Her heart was pounding, and her breathing became shallow. She could hear footsteps coming down the hallway, and voices could be heard speaking in German, which Dora understood perfectly. A soldier could be heard reprimanding someone who had not followed orders about searching the first floor apartments. Dora froze as she realized that the soldiers had overlooked searching the first floor. She held Rose against her as she sat in the hole waiting for their door to be opened.

At that very moment, their apartment door flung open and two SS soldiers entered the room. They turned over chairs, and tables and banged on walls and searched for anything looked suspicious. After they were satisfied that there was nothing was found, they turned to exit the apartment. Suddenly one of the soldiers stopped at the foot or door leading to the hallway. "Quiet," as he stepped back inside the room. He slowly walked another step. He heard a faint whimper coming from the room. Both soldiers stood in silence waiting to hear another sound. Dora had her hand over Rose's mouth, attempting to keep her quiet. There was silence. She heard a tapping sound coming from above. It was the tapping of the soldier's rifle on the floor to see if he could find a hollow space between the floorboards. It took only a moment for the Germans to find the space which led to the spider hole. They lifted up the rug and moved away the table to find a small door on the floor. One of the soldiers took out his flashlight while the other opened the small door. As the soldier beamed his flashlight down into the hole, he saw two small faces looking up at them in terror. Dora was crying, while Rose held her mother tight and began to cry. **"OUT, GET OUT!"**, the German yelled. Dora, climbed out first, then turned to pickup her daughter and wrapped her arms around her. **"GIVE ME THE CHILD,"** the soldier demanded. **"NO"** Dora yelled, holding back her tears, "This is my daughter, my life, she will not be taken from me, **NEVER!!"** He raised his voice again, **"GIVE ME THAT CHILD, I SAID, OR I WILL KILL THE BOTH OF YOU!"** Dora screamed back **"YOU CAN'T TAKE HER, SHE IS INNOCENT, SHE DID NOTHING WRONG! TAKE ME, BUT LEAVE HER ALONE."** The soldier's face became red, and his eyes widened. He quickly approached the two and after a brief struggle grabbed Rose out of Dora's arms. Dora became hysterical, she ran over to the soldier and tried to take Rose out of his clutches. He resisted and pushed her away. **"YOU CANNOT TAKE HER, SHE IS ONLY A CHILD, TAKE ME, NOT HER!!"**

The soldier turned and walked towards the door... Rose now screaming and kicking, **"MOMMY, MOMMY",** reached out her hand, but Dora couldn't reach her. Suddenly, Dora felt a sharp pain on the side of her head. The second soldier hit Dora with the butt of his rifle, and she dropped to the floor unconscious. The two solders left the building. Rose was gone.

Dora was still unconscious as Sam and Regina came out of their apartment a few minutes later to see Dora lying on the floor. They carried her back into her apartment and laid her on her bed. Regina quickly soaked a towel and put it on Dora's head, which was bleeding. It was not long after Regina attended to Dora's wound that David came through the door. He looked at the devastation of the room and quickly yelled, **"WHAT HAPPENED? WHERE IS ROSE?"** He walked to the bed where Dora was lying, still in a semi-conscious state, a huge gash on the side of her head. "Dora, what happened?", David asked. "Where is Rose?" Dora, still dazed by the blow, was in shock and couldn't speak. He looked at his neighbors standing a few feet away, Regina was in tears. Sam stood silent. David no longer asked; he knew. He sat down on the side of the bed, looking down at Dora, tears in his eyes. He picked her up in his arms and held her... they cried.

Later that evening, Rose, along with approximately 1600 other children under the age of 12, were executed at the Ninth Fort outside the Kovno Ghetto. The raid took place over two days, March 27th and 28th, 1944, and was officially designated as Die Kinder-Aktion, (The Children's Action). The directive from German headquarters was to search and remove all the children, the sick and elderly and transport them to the Ninth Fort for execution. Soon after the raid, the ghetto was converted to the Kauen Concentration Camp, and was then liquidated by the Germans. (1)

FOOTNOTES:

(1)Schalkowsky, Samuel (2014-04-14)
The Clandestine History of the Kovno Jewish Ghetto Police:

By Anonymous Members of the Kovno Jewish Ghetto Police. Indiana University Press.
ISBN 978-0-253-01297-5

PHOTO:
Still photograph from the Soviet Film of the liberation of Auschwitz, taken by the film unit of the First Ukrainian Front, shot over a period of several months beginning on January 27, 1945.

PHOTO CREDIT: In the Public Domain. USHMM/Belarusian State Archive of Documentary Film and Photography. Author Alexander Voronzow. http://collections. ushmm.org/search/catalog/pa 14532

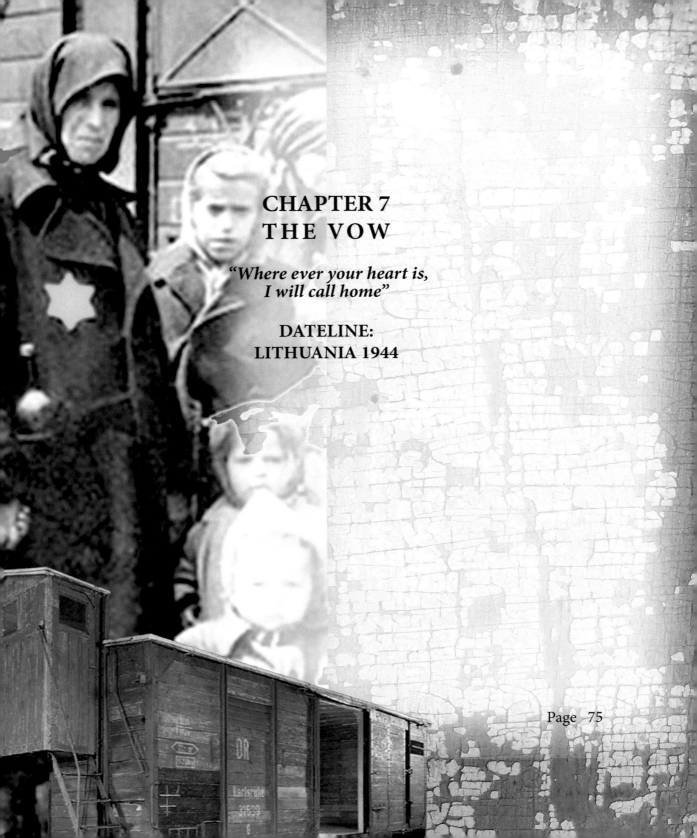

CHAPTER 7
THE VOW

*"Where ever your heart is,
I will call home"*

**DATELINE:
LITHUANIA 1944**

PHOTO
Auschwitz Concentration Camp arrival
of Hungarian Jews Summer, 1944

PHOTO SPREAD:
Deportation to Concentration Camp

PHOTO CREDIT:
Wiki-media Commons by the German Federal Archive of the Cooperation Project. Licensed
under the Creative Commons Attribution Share Alike 3.0 Germany. link: creativecomons.org//
licenses/by-SA/3.0/ck/deed

CHAPTER 7
THE VOW

"Where ever your heart is, I will call home"

DATELINE: LITHUANIA 1944

In July 1944, three months after the death of Rose, David and Dora remained numb over the loss of their daughter. Neither one hardly slept or ate, reliving the nightmare over and over again. The Kovno Ghetto, which had been converted to the Kauen Concentration Camp, was now executing Jews on a mass scale. Of the 30,000 Jews who had lived in Kovno before the war, approximately 3000 remained. By the first week of July, Russian troops had closed in on the rest of Lithuania and the other Baltic countries, retaking the land they had lost only a few years earlier. Many German troops on the battlefield knew the war was lost, but Hitler refused to accept what was happening on the ground. The Generals did not oppose the Fuhrer, knowing full well that they would be shot for treason, if they made even a mention of a withdrawal or surrender.

The High-Command in Berlin, fearing they would be held accountable to the world for their atrocities in the death camps began deporting Jews to other concentration camps away from advancing Allied forces. This action was also taken so the camp's Generals could destroy the evidence, while still keeping the Jews alive for slave labor and subsequent execution.

As the Nazis continued mass house searches for hidden Jews for execution or deportation the Germans began liquidating the Kauen camp (formally the Kovno Ghetto). Those who tried to hide in their housing units were eliminated by the SS by setting their homes a blaze or destroying them with hand grenades.

With approximately 3000 Jews remaining for resettlement, the men were assigned to the Dachau concentration camp in Germany, while the women and children were designated for the Stuffhof concentration camp, in Poland. All were to be deported by train. David, Dora and Sara were the last group to board the trains. No one boarding the trains knew where they were headed. All they were told was that they were being resettled for their safety.

As SS troops assembled their captives in the city square, they began marching them towards awaiting trains. (1), (2) Very few personal belongings were allowed aboard the trains due to the space requirement inside the boxcars.

As David and Dora were part of the last group to reach the railroad platform, they saw many of the war-weary prisoners being herded onto the cattle cars. Many screamed that they couldn't move. Some tried to escape but were quickly apprehended and shot. As the couple had only a few minutes to say goodbye, amidst the cacophony of barking dogs, police whistles, and the sharp commands yelled by impatient SS guards, they embraced. David held Dora close, as she shook in fear surrounded by a sea of bewildered deportees heading for the trains The couple knew this could be the last time they would see each other for some time. As the last remaining captives were being forced towards the trains, David whispered in Dora's ear. **"No matter where they take us, we will meet back here in the Square. Stay strong my Love, and know my thoughts and prayers are with you."** Dora replied with tears in her eyes. **"I love you David and I will pray every night that God keeps us safe and brings us back home to each other."** As those last few words were spoken David felt a sharp pain in his back. **"MOVE, MOVE"**, shouted an angry SS Guard, pushing his cold steel rifle in his backside. **"GET GOING"** as he continued to ram the end of his rifle into David's back, pushing David and Dora apart. As they began walking to their awaiting trains, they looked back one last time and gave a slight wave as they both got swept away by the crowds of people being pushed onto the boxcars.

FOOTNOTES:

1. The dimensions of the cattle cars were approximately 27 feet by 7 feet, and each car was loaded with over 200 people, way beyond capacity. As the doors were shut, those inside started screaming about the conditions. For the next 6 hours they were placed in a "rolling coffin" headed for a living hell. Most had to stand, as there was no room to sit because of the severe overcrowding. Some had their hands straight in the air because they could not move if they put their hand down. There was little ventilation, and the heat was unbearable, as the temperature rose above 100 degrees inside. The Germans didn't care and they did not provide the deportees with any food or water throughout their long journey. The only sanitary provisions was one bucket for the occupants. Many died from suffocation or heart attacks before they reached their final destination. The united States Holocaust Museum; Holocaust encyclopedia. German Railrays and the Holocaust.

2. The European rail network played a crucial role during the Holocaust as millions of Jews were deported by rail to camps throughout Europe as Germany's "Final Solution". The Germans attempted to disguise their deadly intentions, referring to these deportations as "resettlement to the east." The victims were told they were being taken to labor camps to work for the Reich, but in reality, from 1942 on, deportation for most Jews meant death.

Deportations on such a massive scale required the coordination of numerous German government ministries including the Reich Security Office, the Transport Ministry, and the Foreign Office. These government departments coordinated and directed the deportations; organized train schedules; and in some instances the Foreign Office negotiated with German-allied countries to handover of "their Jews" to the Nazis.

One of the most ironic events of the war was that most of the Jews were forced to pay for their own deportations, particularly wherever passenger carriages were used. These payments came in the form of direct money deposit to the SS in exchange for the "resettlement to work in the East" lie. Adults selected for deportation were being charged full price for their one-way ticket, while children under 12 years of age paid half price and children under the age of 4 traveled free. Those who were running out of money in the ghetto were loaded onto trains first for deportation to the concentration camps as they were the first to die, while those with some remaining supplies of gold and cash were shipped last. In reality, the Jews were paying for their own demise.

The SS and the German government offices pocked most of the money that was primarily paid in cash. The receipts taken for mass deportations between 1938 to 1945 reached a sum total of US $664,525,820.34. Wikipedia; Holocaust Trains; the Role of Railways in the Final Solution.

PHOTO:
One of the trains that left Bergen-Belsen for Theresienstadt in early April, 1945, liberated by American Forces.

PHOTO CREDIT:
In Public Domain, US Army soldier took photo as part of his duties for the United States.

PHOTO: A 35- year old woman from the Hungarian town of Mako and her 5-year old daughter, liberated near the German village of Farsleben from a train taking concentration camp inmates from Bergen-Belsen to another camp further east.

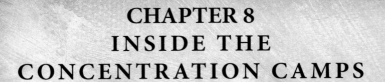

CHAPTER 8
INSIDE THE
CONCENTRATION CAMPS

"Time there is not like it is here on earth…
The inhabitants of this [other] planet had no names,
they had no parents nor did they have children…
They breathed according to different laws of
nature, they did not live – nor did they die –
according to the laws of this world.
Their name was the number."

Ka-Tzetnik (Yechiel Dinur)

DATELINE:
STUTTHOF CC; (STUTTHOF, POLAND), /
DACHAU (MUNICH, GERMANY) -1944 - 1945

PHOTO SPREAD:
Death Camp- Auschwitz Birkenau in /German occupied
Poland (1940-1945)

PHOTO CREDIT:
Yad Vashem, Jerusalem Auschwitz Album, Public Domain

CHAPTER 8
INSIDE THE CONCENTRATION CAMPS

"Time there is not like it is here on earth... The inhabitants of this [other] planet had no names, they had no parents nor did they have children... They breathed according to different laws of nature, they did not live – nor did they die – according to the laws of this world. Their name was the number."

Ka-Tzetnik (Yechiel Dinur)

DATELINE:
STUTTHOF CC; (STUTTHOF, POLAND), /
DACHAU (MUNICH, GERMANY) -1944 - 1945

Dora and Sara arrived at the Stutthof Concentration Camp, in northern Poland, on July 11th, 1944, while David arrived at Dachau, northwest of Munich, Germany, several days later. The three barely survived the journey due to the unbearable conditions aboard the "death trains."

Stutthof Camp located near Danzig, Poland, was erected in 1936 in a secluded, damp, wooded area not far from the Baltic Sea. Initially run as a civilian internment camp under the Danzig police department, the camp was converted into a concentration camp in January 1942, when Poland had already been occupied by German forces. To accommodate the large numbers of Jews and others who were captured by the Nazis in Poland, Hitler and his Generals enlarged the facility and ran its operation by the Nazi SS who were solely responsible for enforcing racial policy. In the following year, the camp was enlarged again to include 38 wooden barracks and housed a total population of men, women and children of nearly 110,000 from 25 different countries at the height of its operation. This included 40 sub-camps surrounding the main camp which was expanded to 1.2 miles.

Stutthof staff consisted of several Camp Commanders, a large contingency of German SS guards, a staff of medical personnel and a camp foreman and helpers to maintain the facility. In late 1943, Ukrainian pro-Nazi guards replaced many of the German guards who were re-assigned to the eastern front to fight the resurgent Russian forces. In addition to the Ukrainians joining ranks with the Germans, Germany added female guards to many camps throughout Europe, including the Stuttoff complex of camps where 295 Nazi women guards were deployed.

A crematorium and gas chamber were added in 1943, which coincided with the startup of mass execution in Stutthof and other camps across Europe. Mobile gas wagons were also used to increase the capacity of executions due to the influx of prisoners coming from Poland, Ukraine, and the Baltic countries (Lithuania, Latvia, Estonia), most being Jews, Catholics, gypsies and rebel resistance fighters.

The driving force for most Nazis during the rampage and killings of the local populous throughout Europe was a Nazi ideological principal called **LEBENSRAUM**. This insane ideology gave justification for the Nazis to aggressively pursue German territorial expansion in central and Eastern Europe for colonization. Simply put, Germany would have more living space for the Aryan Race, which Hitler called the **"Master Race."** And to achieve this goal, they ordered the roundup of millions of innocent people throughout Europe in order to placed them into "killing centers." Such areas were called ghettos and concentration camps which were used for extermination through starvation, poor living conditions, disease, and mass executions, among other sinister methods.

Page 86

CHAPTER 8: INSIDE THE CONCENTRATION CAMPS

The day Dora and Sara arrived,from their 9 hour journey, they were told to shower and de-louse. They were given prison clothes and furnished with a bunk bed, made of paper mattresses, pillows filled with wood shavings, and a blanket made of cotton material. The barracks had no heat or hot water. Inside the hut shaped barracks there housed over 200 women which was designed for less than 100. The living conditions were primitive. The barracks included a double row of bunk beds, several small sinks and 4 toilets which were unusable. Rags were used for toilet paper, if you were lucky. The freezing temperatures at night and the stench were unimaginable. A few hours of sleep was the norm for most prisoners during their captivity.

The camp's population was served rations of bread, horse meat soup and a small potato, doled out a few times a week. Although many of the new arrivals died during the initial stage of entering the camp, Dora and Sara and were assigned to a work detail outside the camp to dig anti-tank ditches. These ditches were dug 6 feet deep and 3 feet wide for miles around the perimeter of the camp which the Germans believed would impede advancing Russian troops from the east. The sisters' workday was brutal, working 6 days a week, 16-hour days. Many days they could hardly walk, or even move their hands, which were raw and bloodied from hours of continuous shoveling with their bare hands...

One of the tenets of the Nazi plan (**"The Final Solution"**) was to kill all the Jews by working them to death. Those who first entered the camp and deemed to be too sick or weak to work were immediately ushered into the "so-called showers" which the prisoners thought would cleanse them from days spent inside the overcrowded and stifling boxcars. Instead, people were gassed to death inside the shower room by poisonous gas pellets dropped from the ceiling above. Once the shower doors were opened, prisoners removed the bodies, dragging them to the crematorium area for disposal. Victims included men, women and children. Others died more slowly through starvation, disease or sheer exhaustion from working 16 hour days and little sleep.

On January 12,1945, the Russian army began their Winter Counter Offensive pushing the Germans further back from occupied territory which had conquered only several years earlier. With the advancement of Russian troops towards Poland, Stutthof's Camp Generals decided to initiate an evacuation plan to move the captives to other camps closer to Germany in order to keep the Jews working for Germany's **"war machine"**, while systemically working the Jews to death to maintain their goal of **"ethnic cleansing"**.

On 26th January 1945, the Commandant of the Stutthof Camp ordered to commence with the evacuation of the camp by transporting prisoners to other camps in order to destroy any evidence of atrocities that took place inside the camp over its six years of existence. The deportation initiative was to march nearly 25,000 prisoners (mostly Jews), to the Baltic Sea, over 20 miles away, to awaiting barges that would carry them to Germany for resettlement.

The march, called the **"Death March to the Sea"** took 7-8 days to complete. Those who were selected formed marching columns, in groups of 500-1000 people, guarded by SS soldiers who were ordered to shoot to kill anyone who tried to escape during the march or lagged behind. One of the last groups to leave the camp included Dora and her Sister. The evacuation totaled almost half of the total population of the camp at the time, leaving 24,000 prisoners still remaining in the camp.

Those who marched were given a few blankets and camp clothes, as well as provisions of around 500 grams of bread, some margarine, or processed cheese. Most of the starving prisoners immediately ate all the food during the early stages of the march, only to starve to death later, since rations were doled out only sporadically throughout the march. The march was brutal as the columns of prisoners walked through deep snow in temperatures of -20° C along with howling winds and blowing snow. Frequently they marched into the night, and stopped in places that were chosen randomly including barns, cowsheds and churches. Once the groups reached the coastline, they were ordered to swim out in the icy cold water in order to reach the barges that were anchored several hundred feet from the coastline. Those too weak or could not swim were immediately machine-gunned in the icy waters of the Baltic Sea by SS soldiers stationed along the shoreline. Many others who reached the barges soon died due to exposure.

Dora and Sara were in the final group to march from the Stuttoff camp, and faced extreme conditions as the snow drifts were so high that walking became almost impossible. The blowing snow and the plummeting temperatures also made the journey beyond the capabilities of many on the March. Many died along the way and were left in the snow. As day six started, after sleeping in a Church that night before, the final group of half-frozen prisoners where barely able to move their feet. Nearing their destination of the frigid waters of the Baltic, frostbite had already set in for most. Those who still remained alive, including the Sisters reached a point where their will to live was almost gone.. Dora, now in excruciating pain looked over at Sara who was next to her, barely able to speak due to ice forming around her mouth. **"Sara, I don't think I'm going to make it, my feet are frozen and my legs can hardly move."** Sara, feeling the pain in her own limbs, replied, **"we have to keep going, sister, we have no choice. If we fall, we'll die! Look! The ocean is not far."** Dora's tears, frozen to her face, looked ahead but could only see those in front of her. The pain was consuming her. Marching so long in such extreme conditions, with little food or sleep was finally overtaking her body. Death seemed almost inevitable. There was nothing left inside. One of the Guards noticed the Sisters slowing their pace, and yelled, **"KEEP MOVING YOU TWO, YOU ARE NOT KEEPING UP...MOVE!, MOVE!, I WILL NOT TELL YOU AGAIN."** The Sisters knew if they stopped, even for a moment, it would be the last step they would ever take. As the marchers turned on the road leading towards the sea, the ocean was in sight. Dora's legs started to buckle again. She knew she couldn't go much further before she would fall. **"Sara, I can't make it."** At that very moment, the sound of marching feet was broken by loud popping noise in the distance. From the tree line, came a platoon of soldiers running towards the group, their rifles blazing. They were Russian soldiers in spread formation, yelling as they ran. The group of around 150 weary frozen marchers and a dozen or so Nazi guards hit the ground to avoid the bullets flying passed them. Two of the Germans were immediately hit along with several marchers. Totally taken by surprise the remaining Nazi guards crawled along the snowy ground and were able to reach the tree line on the opposite side of road. As they took positions, they returned fire, hitting several Russian soldiers who fell to the ground. There ensued a vicious exchange of rifle and machine gun fire, between the two groups of soldiers from opposite sides of the road, with the prisoners caught in the crossfire, their heads buried in the snow. While bullets whistled passed them from both directions, the marchers dare not move an inch, afraid they would be hit by flying bullets just feet from their frozen bodies. The battle was short but fierce, as German and Russian soldiers continued to exchange fire. Some of the marchers could be heard yelling out, as bullets pierced their tattered jackets, while others were screaming in fear. Then, the shooting stopped.

Among the fatalities were 4 Prisoners, 3 Russian Soldiers, 12 Nazi Guards. In addition 6 Prisoners; along with 2 Russians were wounded. Once the fighting ended the Russian soldiers picked up the Marchers from the ground and huddled them along the tree line. The snow was beginning to fall again. Dora, Sara and the others were given heavy blankets and hot coffee from the rations the Russians brought with them. Some of the Marchers were dazed and in shock while others were crying uncontrollably. The Sisters just sat there, motionless, expressionless. During the entire ordeal their faces were pinned down into the snow.

It was not long before Russian military trucks arrived to take them to a nearby Russian outpost where they received temporary medical attention before being transported to a nearby hospital. Dora and Sara who sustained serious frostbite on their legs and feet as well as severe dehydration and malnutrition were also given treatment. Of the 500+ marchers who set out on the 26 mile **"death"** march from the Stuttoff Concentration Camp to the Baltic Sea in 1945, less than 200 survived. Their long-awaited liberation from the Nazi onslaught had finally come to an end. The two sisters cried as they were driven away from the road leading to the Baltic Sea. A road that would have led to certain death. But through the Grace of God, the two were finally safe and grateful to be alive.

It was estimated of the 25,000 prisoners who participated in the **"Death March,"** from the Stutthof Concentration Camp to the Baltic Sea one in two died during the March or later died in other concentration camps before liberation. (1)

DAVID - DACHAU CONCENTRATION CAMP:

When David arrived at Dachau on July,12, 1944, a day after Dora and Sara arrived at Stutthof, the conditions were beyond comprehension. Dachau, in the early years of Hitler's rise to power, was the first concentration camp to become operational in 1933. It was also the camp that existed the longest, from March 1933 until April 1945, which was nearly all twelve years of the Nazi regime. Dachau's close proximity to Munich where Hitler and his Nazi party established their official headquarters in 1933, made the location quite convenient for Nazi officials and Hitler himself, although he never stepped foot inside the Camp once it was operational.

Conditions at the camp, like all of the camps were brutal and overcrowded. The facility had been originally designed to house some 6,000 detainees, but the population continued to rise as more and more Jews and others, including Allied soldiers were captured. By the time David arrived in 1944, the number of prisoners exceeded 30,000, almost five times the number the camp was designed to house, making life inside the camp unbearable.

Daily life inside the camp was beyond comprehension. Prisoners were used as forced slave labor, working up to 18 hours days on various construction and weapon production projects. Many of the women and children were forced to work on small handicraft projects which subsequently purchased by local merchants who sold the items to the public. Prisoners were also given hard labor which included building roads, draining marshes, and working on other armament production factories outside the camp for Germany's war effort. Thousands were worked to death.

When David arrived in Dachau, he was assigned to forced labor at an aircraft manufacturing plant outside the gates of the camp. There he produced aircraft parts and other materials for Germany's air-force. (Luftwaffe). On certain days, he was also forced to work nights as an electrician for the camp's maintenance department. As part of his job he was responsible for inspecting and repairing the camp's electrical fences. This job included the ghoulish task of removing dead bodies of detainees who had committed suicide by throwing themselves against the barbed wired electrical fences or those who attempted to escape.

Within the camp, human medical experiments were performed on a regular basis by Nazi physicians and medical staff on large numbers of prisoners, including children. Prisoners were forced to participate without consent, including experimental surgery without anesthesia which resulted in trauma, disfiguration and sometimes death.

As more and more prisoners arrived each day, most knew that Dachau was nothing more than a place where people were turned into slaves and worked to death or otherwise died from conditions inside the camp.

In the winter of 1944-1945, Europe was experiencing one of the coldest winters on record. Most of the Germany knew that the days of the 3rd Reich was coming to a close as Allied forces were quickly closing in on German strongholds inside of major German cities. Yet, resettlement of the Jews continued, as trains from other camps continued to arrive into Dachau daily without disruption. Hitler and his inner circle were obsessed to continue killing Jews regardless of what was happening on the battlefield. As more and more prisoners arrived, an outbreak of typhus fever spread throughout the camp, killing thousands. The prisoners who were strong enough continued to work, although their numbers dwindled, due to disease. The numbers of deaths became so unmanageable that many of the dead were removed from the camp and buried in large pits outside the gates, rather than cremation. The sheer number of dead bodies had accumulated far beyond the capacity than the crematorium could process. Eventually, prisoner trains arriving daily from other ghettos were left outside camp grounds without ever opening the doors. There was no room inside the camp to house them. Countless numbers died inside locked train cars from the elements, suffocation or starvation.

As the Allied forces advanced towards Germany and Dachau, Hitler and his Generals gave the orders to begin an evacuation of prisoners of Dachau to Southern Germany, where they could continue working at other camps. Such **"Death March"** evacuations became a normal procedure toward the end of the war, as it gave the Germans the opportunity to destroy evidence of their atrocities inside the camp, while keeping prisoners working and dying.

On April 24,1945, just prior to liberation of Dachau by the Allied forces, SS guards began marching some 7000 prisoners including David towards the Southern German-Austrian border, 37 miles away. The prisoners were led in columns on side roads which were difficult to travel due to the terrain and weather. During the six-day march, anyone who could not keep up was shot on the spot while others died of exposure, hunger or exhaustion. During the final days of the march the U.S. Army's 522 Field Artillery Battalion spotted the marchers along with SS Guards. The quickly took positions along the roadway inside the tree line, rifles locked and loaded. The commanding Officer waited for the marchers to draw nearer to the Americans who were poised to shoot, when he yelled out to the Germans to drop their weapons. The 20 or so guards, startled, looked around and saw they were surrounded by heavily armed American G. I.s. They knew they didn't have a chance. There was no resistance by the German soldiers. They immediately dropped their weapons and surrendered. The marchers including David were finally free.

During the march dozens of the marchers died of hunger, exposure or exhaustion. David and many other marchers who were fortunate s enough to live were immediately transported into a Red Cross facility for medical attention. David was placed into an ICU section almost immediately for a variety of serious health conditions which included sever malnutrition, severe dehydration, exhaustion, and seriously infected wounds from regular beatings by SS Guards. He also developed a high fever due to his infections. If it were not for the American Soldiers who liberated the group that day, David would probably had died before reaching the Austrian border. Fortunately, with proper medical attention which included strong antibiotics and intravenous feedings his condition improved. (2)

FOOTNOTES:

(1)Death March (holocaust) - Wikipedia the free encyclopedia
https://en.wikipedia.org/wiki/Wikipedia:Text_of_Creative_Commons_Attribution-
ShareAlike_3.0_Unported_License

(2)Dachau Concentration Camp - Wikipedia:Text_of_Creative_Commons_Attribution-
ShareAlike_3.0_Unported_License

PHOTO
Jewish Men are forced to load munitions train under German supervision.

PHOTO CREDIT:
United States Holocaust Memorial Museum, courtesy of National Archives and Records Administration College Park, Maryland.
https://collections. ushmm.org/search/catalog/pa 1036871

PHOTO
Inside Buchenwald Concentration Camp

PHOTO CREDIT:
Public Domain courtesy of Flickr.com
https://www.flickr.com/photos/pingnews/441530476

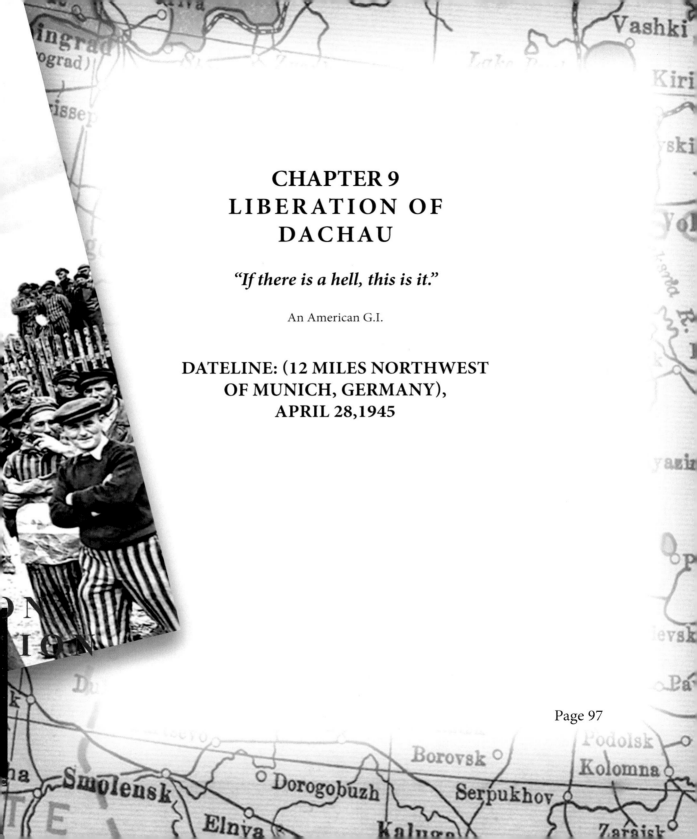

CHAPTER 9
LIBERATION OF DACHAU

"If there is a hell, this is it."

An American G.I.

DATELINE: (12 MILES NORTHWEST OF MUNICH, GERMANY), APRIL 28,1945

PHOTO SPREAD:
After American troops arrived, homemade American flag was raised by the prisoners of Dachau prison camp. As it waved in the breeze, it seemed to reflect the joy of the inmates who realize freedom for the first time in many years. April 30, 1945

PHOTO CREDIT:
United States Holocaust Memorial Museum, Courtesy of National Archives and Records Administration, College Park, Maryland. Photographer: Arland B. Musser. Copyright: Public Domain Source Record ID: 111-SC-207745 (Album 1469).

PHOTO:
General Dwight D. Eisenhower addresses American paratroopers prior to D-Day. "General Dwight D. Eisenhower gives the order of the Day. 'Full victory-nothing else" to paratroopers in England, just before they board their airplanes to participate in the first assault in the invasion of the continent of Europe." Eisenhowe is meeting with US Co. E 502nd Parachute Infantry Regiment (Strike) of the 101st Airborne Division, photo taken at Greenham Common Airfield in England about 8:30 p.m. on June 5, 1944.

PHOTO CREDIT:
Unknown U.S. Army photographer. This image is available from the United States Library of Congress's Prints and Photographs division under the digital ID cph.3a26521 From Wiki-media Commons, the free media repository. Public Domain.

PHOTO:
Soldiers move onto Omaha Beach during the Allied Invasion of Europe on D-Day, June 6, 1944.

Page 100

PHOTO:
42nd Infantry Division liberated infamous Dachau Concentration Camp in 1945.

PHOTO CREDIT:
Col. Richard Goldenberg. DOD (Department of Defense) makes no representations
warranties of any kind regarding the suitability of DOD VI for non-DOD purposes.

PHOTO:
Survivors from a death march from Dachau huddle around a camp fire prepared by
Japanese-American soldiers with the 522nd Field Artillery Battalion. May, 1945

PHOTO CREDIT:
United States Holocaust Memorial Museum, Courtesy of Eric Saul. Public Domain

CHAPTER 9
LIBERATION OF DACHAU

"If there is a hell, this is it."

An American G.I.

DATELINE: (12 MILES NORTHWEST OF MUNICH, GERMANY), APRIL 28,1945

As David was recovering in the ICU outside of Munich, Germany, word spread around the hospital that the Dachau Concentration Camp had been liberated.

On April 29th, 1945, the day started like every other day inside Dachau, as half-dead, starved prisoners were dragged from their barracks at 5 a.m. for roll-call. But this time, the prisoners noticed that the 4 watchtowers guarding the square were empty and there were fewer guards standing in the square for the morning count. Little did the prisoners know that during the middle of the night most of the guards had fled fearing that Allied forces were quickly closing in on camp from the east.

In the meantime an American Scouting Patrol from the U.S. Seventh Army's 45th Infantry Division were deployed ahead of advancing American troops. Their mission was to search for pockets of German resistance troops and detonating land mines. As the small contingency of Americans advanced through the dense woods, they came upon a clearing out of nowhere. As they got closer, they noticed a long stretch of railroad tracks which led to dozens of boxcars in the distance. Moving closer, the soldiers began to smell a strong odor which made it hard for them to breath. The stench was so overpowering, some became weakened and nauseous. As they reached the boxcars, they unlocked the huge doors of one of the cars to find hundreds of skeletal remains of men, women and children lying on the boxcar floor. Some were sprawled on top of one another, while others were lying against the wall as if they were trying to find a way out. They had been dead for days, possibly longer. All had died of suffocation or dehydration. The soldiers were aghast at what they saw. It was unimaginable to see human beings killed in such a grotesque and horrific manner. There will dozens of locked boxcars found that morning which held more then 2,000 remains. The G.I.s who came upon the locked boxcars that day would never be the same. What they witnessed would haunt them for the rest of their lives.

It was later learned by the American Generals that the German Commanders knew before the trains even arrived, that they couldn't accommodate more prisoners due to overcrowding. As a result, they decided the thousands of men, women and children mostly. Jews, would remain inside the stifling boxcars to die.

Later that day, the United States 45th Infantry Division entered the gates to Dachau with little resistance. Most of the Nazi soldiers overseeing the camp were gone, leaving only a hundred or so Nazis soldiers to hold the facility. Few Germans resisted as American forces arrived. Those who did resist were quickly eliminated by the Americans.

As the American soldiers streamed through the gates of the camp, they discovered more than 62,000 remaining prisoners, barely alive of which 13,000 died later from malnutrition and disease.

As American forces along with 5 Star General Dwight D. Eisenhower entered the main housing units of Dachau, they were greeted by the welcoming prisoners. Many wept watching the soldiers entering the camp, while others grabbed and kissed the hands of the marching soldiers. They were overwhelmed with emotion. They waited so long for this day, the day of their liberation. Even some of the battled-hardened G.Is had tears in their eyes as they marched through the complex. What the soldiers witnessed that day was beyond human comprehension. So many prisoners throughout the grounds were just skin and bones, others were lying on the ground, dead or dying.

The smell of decaying bodies and human excrement was everywhere as the soldiers moved deeper into the main area of the camp. Some had been dead for hours, others for days One group of soldiers entered a part of the complex that contained a row of concrete structures that contained rooms full of hundreds of naked and barely clothed dead bodies piled on to wheel barrels and carts. Next to the structures was a coal-fired crematorium that was still burning. In the same area, G.Is found large shower stalls where prisoners were suppose to shower before being assigned housing, but instead the showers were filled with poison gas. Their lifeless bodies were found on the ground along side the crematorium. The conditions throughout the camp were beyond the soldiers' worst nightmare, As one G.I. commented to his Sergeant as they surveyed the grounds, **"If there is a hell, this is it."** Proper sanitation throughout the camp was practically non-existent. There was no running water inside the prisoner facilities. The few rations which still remained were mostly spoiled or consumed by rats.

It did not take long before American medics went into action. They quickly brought in hundreds of stretchers and cots and began attending to the sick and dying. Dozens of prisoners were transported to nearby medical facilities outside the camp. Unfortunately, many died while being attended to. Additional troops from the 42nd Infantry constructed a fully functioning makeshift hospital on the campgrounds and bought in generators and fresh water. It took only two days for a second hospital to be functional, using the Nazi barracks. Liberated inmates who were strong enough worked alongside American troops to do what they could to help those who needed medical attention. The liberation of Dachau was bitter-sweet for both the Americans and the survivors. And will certainly never be forgotten.

During the years of Dachau's existence, there were more than 216,000 registered prisoners from more than 30 countries who entered the gates of Hitler's first concentration camp, Dachau. Of those, almost 45,000 perished, although historians believe thousands more died during the early years when the camp first opened as well as at the end of the war when "new arrivals" were never registered. The final number of dead will never be known.

(1)

FOOTNOTES:

(1) History.com, The Horrifying discovery of Dachau Concentration Camp and liberation by U.S. Troops, www.history.com/news/dachau-concentration-camp-liberation.

PHOTO:
Polish prisoners in Dachau Nazi concentration camp in Germany joyfully celebrating their liberation by the U.S. Army.

PHOTO CREDIT:
United States Holocaust Memorial Museum (https://www.ushmn.org), photograph No. 83818. National Archives and Records Administration, College Park. Source Record ID: 111-SC-207743

PHOTO:
Young and old survivors in Dachau cheer approaching U.S. troops.

PHOTO CREDIT
Courtesy of National Archives and Records Admiistration, College Park, Maryland.
United States Holocaust Memorial Museum, Photograph No. 45075.

CHAPTER 10
THE MISSION

"Courage is not having the strength to go on;
it is going on
when you don't have the strength."

Theodore Roosevelt

DATELINE:
MUNICH, GERMANY, APRIL, 1945

PHOTO SPREAD:
Man walking on the
road. Public Domain.

PHOTO SPREAD:
The Destroyed Railway
Station of Saint-Lo.
(Normandy) destroyed
summer 1944

PHOTO CREDIT:
Conseil Regional de
Basse-Normandie/
National Archives USA
Creative Commons
CCO License
A Hribution Share Alike
license 3.0

CHAPTER 10
THE MISSION

"Courage is not having the strength to go on; it is going on when you don't have the strength."

Theodore Roosevelt

DATELINE:
MUNICH, GERMANY, APRIL, 1945

David's recovery progressed much faster than the doctors expected. It took only a few weeks before he regained most of his strength and his ability to walk again without much pain. He was determined to follow doctor's orders and move through recovery as quickly as possible. He had no time to be lying in a hospital bed when he had such a critical "mission" of returning to Kaunas to reunite with his wife. What concerned him more than Dora's whereabouts was whether she was even alive. And even if she was, did she have enough strength to make it back to Kaunas. She very well could be in a hospital or displacement camp somewhere in Europe, just trying to stay alive.

While in recovery David decided to map out a route that would take him through a number of displacement camps on his journey back to Kaunas and Dora. He knew his route home would be dangerous, but he didn't want to take the chance of not searching for her along the way. She could be anywhere, if she was still alive. He was committed to follow his plan.(1)

David's strength improved over the days ahead and he soon felt strong enough to begin his search, although he wasn't certain his body could withstand the rigors of traveling. Yet, he was determined to begin his mission and asked the Hospital Administrator for an early release. Most of the medical staff had serious reservations about his request for an early release since they felt he still needed more time to recuperate. Nevertheless, David ultimately was able to convince the Hospital Administrator to grant him a discharge, which was granted, albeit reluctantly.

On the day of his release, he was asked to stop by the Hospital Administrator's office for last minute instructions on traveling. He entered the Administrator's office and greeted him along with a few of the doctors from his medical team. "Good Morning David. How are you feeling?", the Hospital Administrator asked. David replied with a big smile, "Feeling fine Doc, today's the big day, I guess." The HA smiled and said, "Come sit down, Dr. Frankel, Dr. Hogan and I would like to talk you about precautions you need to take while traveling." The doctors proceeded to list a number of procedures he needed to follow should he start feeling any chest pain or dizziness. He was also given a supply of antibiotics just in case he needed them. After the briefing, they all shared their good-byes and wished him well on his search. Just as David was ready to leave, the HA reached into his physician's coat pocket and pulled out an envelope. "Just a second David, you may need this." David was handed an envelope and proceeded to open it. He removed a leather covered document folder with the United Nations emblem embossed on the front cover. David eyes grew wide. "What is this Doc?", David asked. "Well David, what you have in your hands few people rarely receive. It's actually a special UN pass from the United Nations Tracing Committee allowing you to pass through multiple borders, in order to enter any displacement camp on your own without getting prior authorization.(2). "All you have to do is show the pass to the Camp Administrator when you enter the grounds." David was elated, he was at a loss for words. "Thanks Doc, I can't tell you how much this means to me. This will surely make my journey a lot easier. I can't thank you enough for all you've done." They all shook hands. "We'll be thinking of you David; the best of luck." They all smiled.

It was remarkable that David was granted such a high-level pass, since in most cases permission to travel without restrictions was only granted to government officials/ diplomats, military personnel or medical staff. The Hospital Administrator obviously knew people very high in the chain of command.

David's first stop was to meet with a UN Observer who was assigned to the UN hospital where David stayed during his weeks in recovery. They grew to know each other quite well over that time. They sat in a small office in the back of the hospital and began mapping out a route east/northeast from Munich, which would take David through parts of Germany, Czechoslovakia, Poland and finally Lithuania. The U.N. Observer also pinpointed the locations of the newly constructed U.N. Relief Displacement Camps along his route. Identifying locations of DP camps was important. First, it gave David temporary shelter to rest and just as important, to see if Dora was in the camp or had been there. With U.N. pass in hand, David left the hospital. As he departed from the building he realized he was a "free man" for the first time in nearly five years of captivity inside the ghetto and Dachau. He could breathe again without looking over his shoulder for fear of being threatened or beaten by SS guards.

To his fortune, as he turned the corner on the way to the bus station, a U.N. delivery truck was leaving the hospital and suddenly stopped to see if David needed a ride. It turned out they were both heading in the same direction. He jumped aboard and thought, "This could be a good omen".

It was late afternoon before David arrived in Nuremberg, Germany, 150 miles from where he began. Nuremberg was a small town in Bavaria which housed a temporary Displacement Camp (DP) of 1500 people. David realized the trip had taken longer than expected and the drive made him very tired. The hour was getting late when he arrived. He was welcomed into the camp by the Camp Director and several UN soldiers, who offered him a cot in one of the tents. Exhausted, David soon fell asleep, believing that God was with him and prayed that Dora was still alive.

The next morning David was feeling much better. He had a hearty breakfast with a few camp administrators, discussing his "mission". Unfortunately, he learned from camp officials that there were no registered people from Lithuania inside their camp. Most of the residents in Nuremberg were from Germany, Austria, and Czechoslovakia. The mix of nationalities from eastern Europe including Lithuania would be vastly greater as David headed east. Not discouraged, David moved on that afternoon. He had known from the outset that the search would be daunting.

The displacement camp at Nuremberg was the first of over a dozen DP camps David visited on his route across Germany, Czechoslovakia, Poland and Lithuania. As his search continued from camp to camp, there was no one who knew any Lithuanians who were registered. David did all he could to stay positive and conserve his energy. There were times he thought he couldn't go on. Walking became difficult, and getting enough rest and nourishment was challenging. Nevertheless, he pushed on, believing he would find Dora on his route or waiting for him in Kaunas. He slept where he could, whether in barns or churches and if he was really fortunate, he ran into charitable people who offered him a place to sleep and a meal in their homes. On one occasion, he was roughed up by several local "villagers" in a small town in Germany who didn't take kindly to strangers, especially after the war. Fortunately, he escaped without serious injury.

The search was long and arduous, as days turned into weeks. David traveled day and night, by any mode of transportation he could find. Whether by car, truck, train, or sometimes foot, his goal was just to reach his next DP camp. Occasionally, an American G.I. or Allied soldier would pick him up along the roadside and give him a ride to the next town or village. When he arrived, most of the "locals" in the towns just ignored him. He was an "outsider", a refugee, who had no place in their community. To them, any stranger drew suspicion. There was an incident in a small Czechoslovakian town when David was accused of being a Nazi spy. He was surrounded by a group of young men on the street who tied him up inside a barn and tried to get a confession from him by threating to cut his throat. When he wouldn't confess, they left him there overnight, his hands and feet tied to a chair. The next morning the men returned and let him go after he showed proof that he had permission to travel through their country. An incident he would not forget.

As time passed and his journey became more and more difficult, he began to forget what country he was in, as many of the camps started looking the same. The only way he could distinguish one camp from another was by the language the "locals" were speaking. The stress of traveling was now taking a toll on him my mentally and physically. He traveled through town after town: Scheinfeld, Ludwig, Regensburg, Salzburg, Prague, Laurinburg, crossing multiple borders.

As David reached Poland, he hitched a ride with a Polish truck driver he met at a road stop. David was on the verge of exhaustion. The driver invited David to his home for dinner. The driver was sympathetic to David's mission and he knew his wife always made enough food when he returned home from a long haul. David accepted his invitation graciously.

Knowing how tired David was from traveling, the Driver and his wife asked him if he would like to stay the night and get some sleep. They didn't have to ask him twice. He graciously accepted. The next morning, having slept soundly, David thanked the couple for their hospitality and bid them farewell. They all agreed that someday they would meet again, under different circumstances.

Resuming his search, David entered the town of Lodz, Poland, only 550 miles from Kaunas, Lithuania where he prayed she would be when he arrived. The city of Lodz, just south of Warsaw was a leading center in Poland for textile manufacturing including cotton, wool and leather products. Occupied and annexed by the Germans during the early stages of World War II, part of the city was sectored off to house a Ghetto which held approximately 130,000 Jews. Most of the Jewish population were systemically murdered during occupation, as they considered the Jews to be a direct threat to the German people. During the war many areas of the city were destroyed by the fighting between German and Russian forces. The city was finally liberated by the Russians in January, 1945. After the war the residents of Lodz primarily comprised of Poles, Russians and Germans.

As David entered the center of the town, he saw that most of the buildings had been destroyed. Few shops were open, and most people on the street were gathered at a local cafe which was partially opened. After stopping at the café for coffee, he headed toward the DP camp, his hopes now on the rise, not because he believed she would be there, but because he was now less than 250 miles from Kaunas.

As he continued walking towards the camp entrance, he suddenly noticed two men walking towards him conversing in Yiddish, (a language spoken by Jews living in that part of Europe). One of the voices sounded familiar...it was a voice he vaguely recalled from the past. David quickly glanced over at the men as they walked past and thought, "Where have I heard that voice before?" David stopped and turned back to take another look. Without taking another breath, David's voice jubilantly rang out "Sam, is that you?" Sam, startled for a moment, turned to look back and replied, "David? David Ruskin? I can't believe it! Oh my God, you are still alive!" The two men grabbed each other in an impassioned embrace. David showing his excitement said, "Sam, I thought you died when the SS was liquidating the Ghetto!" Sam, equally excited, responded, "I thought you died during the last selection at the city square!" They both laughed. Sam Gertner and his wife Regina were neighbors who lived in the apartment next door when the couples lived in the Ghetto. It was Sam and Regina who carried Dora into her apartment when she was hit in the head by the SS Soldier's rifle, and their daughter Rose was taken away, over a year ago.

Sam proceeded to tell David that he and his wife Regina had escaped Kovno by digging under one of the fences along the side of the compound just before the camp was liquidated. They ran into the woods and joined the rebel partisans to fight the Germans, before being captured and sent to Auschwitz prior to liberation.

As the two men continued their conversation, David told Sam about his liberation from Dachau and about the Mission he was on, hoping to find Dora. David commented, "I've been on the road a long time Sam," as he looked down the road at the DP Camp a short distance away. "I'm not sure how much further I can go." David continued, "I had no idea how difficult this journey would be. The last time I saw Dora was when she and Sara were being forced onto the trains in Kaunas last year. They could be anywhere. I'm not sure if they're even alive."

Before David could complete another word, Sam wide-eyed and almost in shock, grabbed David by the shoulders, shaking him excitedly. "David, I saw Dora and Sara only a few hours ago. Dora could hardly walk. I asked them where you were, but Sara said they did not know. They just kept walking toward the infirmary, down the street." As Sam was pointing east, David could see in the distance what appeared to be a partially bombed out two-story building. He could barely make out a small banner draped on the front facade which showed a large Red Cross emblem. (3).

David quickly embraced his friend and said "Thanks Sam!, I'll see you later", and he dashed away running towards the infirmary, three blocks away. The 3 short blocks seemed like miles as he weaved around debris, bomb craters and downed electrical wires along the way. He was exuberant yet apprehensive, fearing Dora's condition could be serious and wondering whether she was still alive. His legs felt heavy as he couldn't move fast enough. He finally ran up the wooden stairs to the front entrance.

As he opened the door, he entered a long hallway where pieces of plaster and metal had fallen onto the floor and were swept away to make a pathway. As he continued down the hallway, he noticed a door with a sign reading "Patient Entrance" written in English, Polish and Russian. David opened the door and instantly noticed the unmistakable smell of antiseptic and rubbing alcohol. There in a large room without shades on the windows were rows of beds with dozens of wounded patients being treated for various wounds and conditions. Most were Russian and Polish soldiers along with a handful of Polish civilians.

The nurse who was tending to a patient in the front of the room was a heavyset Polish woman who looked to be in her 40s. She was tending to one to a Polish soldier when David approached. "Excuse me", he said in Polish. The nurse now grabbing a clean towel to wipe her hands, said, "Can I help you?" David replied, "Yes, can you tell me whether there were two women who arrived earlier today for medical attention?" Puzzled, the woman responded, "I am the only nurse on-call this morning and I don't know of any women who registered since I got here. The nurse who was here earlier already left for the day" The nurse quickly turned away to attend to her patient. Dejected, David started walking away. Before he reached the hallway to exit, the nurse abruptly shouted from across the room, "Check the 2nd floor." David, stunned by her outburst, suddenly felt his hopes rise. He turned and quickly walked out of the room to the stairwell that led to the second floor. As he opened the door to the second-floor landing, he noticed the hallway was a mess, much like the floor below, with unswept floors, broken walls, and one light bulb hanging from the splintered ceiling, which offered only some dim light onto the stairwell.

As David made his way down the hallway he noticed a door that was partially opened. He pushed the door open to a large, musty room with rows of empty cots spaced apart which apparently had be used many times before. As he made his way cautiously across the floor, he could see dust in the air which was even more pronounced by the rays of sunlight that were beaming through a dirty windowpane from the back of the room. As he continued to look around, it appeared the room was empty. He turned to exit, feeling a deep sense of disappointment. Suddenly he heard a woman's voice toward the back of the room. As he looked closer, he saw a silhouette of a woman attending to what appeared to be someone lying on a cot. He could barely hear the woman's voice, but as he got closer he could hear her say "The doctor is coming dear, just a few more minutes."

As David got closer to the woman, her voice became more distinct. Still not noticing his presence, David walked towards her. She turned and was startled to see an image of man standing behind her. "Are you the doctor?" she asked. David, now overwhelmed, knew instantly the woman was Sara. "Sara, it's David." His eyes began filling with tears. Sara stunned, looked closer at him. **"OH MY GOD! David, is it you....it is you!" "Yes",** David replied. Sara, stood frozen for a moment trying to breathe from the shock of seeing David alive. Sara calls out, **"You are still alive, my dear God, you are still alive!"** Shaken, David was unable to speak further. He walked up to her and they embraced without saying another word. They were both in tears. Still holding each other, David slowly looked down to see a motionless woman lying on the cot, her eyes closed, and a tattered blanket covering her small frame, and a small pillow under her head. He couldn't tell if she was dead or alive. Her gaunt pale face, and protruding cheekbones made her look ghost-like. As David bent over, he could see the woman was covered with sweat which had dampened the pillow. Her breathing was shallow, and she was burning with fever. He had found Dora and she was dying of typhus. She had the same look on her face as those who had died in Dachau, only months earlier. Sara stepped aside as David moved closer, kneeling down next to her. He took her frail hand gently. **"Dora"**, he softly whispered. Dora stirred a bit, her eyes still closed. David, still kneeling alongside the cot, gently placed his hand on Dora's cheek and gently kissed her as tears gently rolled down his face onto hers. **"It's me, Dora, it's David. I am here, and we're going home, my Love. We're going home."** He slowly bent over the cot and laid his head next to hers.... Her lifeless body began to stir. He knew she was close to death. Suddenly her eyes began to open and she slowly stared up at him. **"David, are we in heaven?"** Stunned by her words, David replies, **"No, my darling, we're alive and I'm taking you home."** David kisses her cheek. She falls back into unconsciousness. Dora, was hallucinating from her fever, thinking David was an angel who came to take her to heaven. Her breathing continued to become more shallow. Overwhelmed with emotion, David and Sara knelt along side of her, trying to hold back their tears.

FOOTNOTES:

1. Displacement Camps after the War

In May 1945, Europe was in shambles. With the fall of Nazi Germany, the Allies had the massive undertaking of rebuilding Europe. The War and its aftermath had uprooted hundreds of thousands of people from their homes throughout Europe. Many liberated from the Nazi concentration camps had no home to return to. As a result, the Allies established, under the umbrella of the United Nations, the United Nations Relief and Rehabilitation Administration. (UNRRA). This organization was solely responsible for overseeing the day to day operations of Displaced Persons Camps (i.e. Displacement Camps) and the well-being of those who needed temporary shelter until their homes could be rebuilt or resettlement could be established. Some of the refugees eventually settled in Europe, mainly Great Britain, France, Spain and Switzerland, while most emigrated to the United States, Palestine (Israel), Canada, South Africa and South America. At least 11 million people were displaced throughout Europe after the war, with a total of 850,000 housed in displacement camps. The camps were pardoned off by 3 separate zones, representing the Allies who governed each zone until 1952. Most housed inside the camps were either former political/military prisoners of war or concentration camp survivors. The Allies officially categorized these refugees as "displaced persons" (DPs) in 1945. Most had no homes to returned to after the war.

2. The International Tracing Service (ITS) in Bad Arolsen, Germany, served the victims of Nazi persecution and their families by documenting their fate after liberation.

The ITS provides information about:

-Germans and non-Germans who were detained in Nazi concentration or work camps or other detention sites from 1933 to 1945.

-Victims of the Holocaust. Non-Germans deployed as forced laborers on the territory of the Third Reich during World War II.

-Displaced persons who, after World War II, were under the care of international relief organizations (UNRRA, IRO). United Nations Relief and Rehabilitation Administration, and International Refugee organization.

-Children (i.e. under 18 years of age at the end of World War II) of persons belonging to the above-mentioned groups and displaced or separated from their parents as a result of the war.

3. After Poland was liberated, Allied forces partnered with the International Red Cross to erect emergency temporary infirmaries and mobile hospital units to care for wounded soldiers and wounded and ill civilians all over Europe. Such facilities were built hastily and often lacked necessary equipment and supplies, but they improved over time as the Allies took more control of the devastated cities to rebuild the infrastructure after the war.

(Holocaust Encyclopedia, United States Holocaust Museum Persons.)

Baltiski
(Baltic Port)
HIIUMA
SAAREMAA
TALLINN
Tapa
Kunda

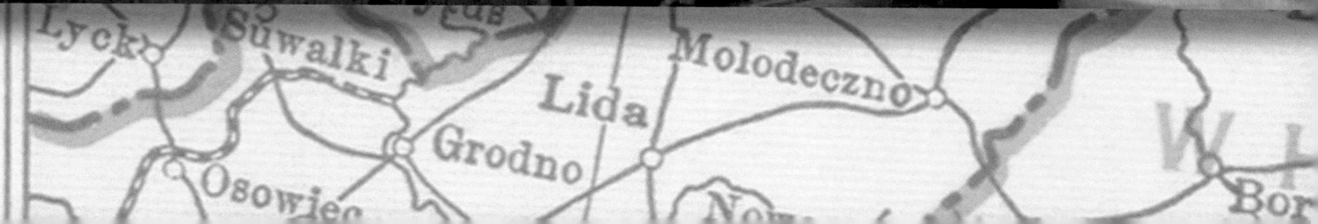
Lyck
Suwalki
Molodeczno
Lida
Grodno
Osowiec

CHAPTER 11
COMING HOME

*"In our darkest hour,
God's light shines the Brightest"*

DATELINE; LODZ, POLAND - 1945

PHOTO SPREAD:
Interior view of Oldway War Hospital, Devon, England

PHOTO CREDIT:
Interior view of Oldway War Hospital, Paignton,
Devonm England, by Aussie-mobs is marked under CCPDM 1.0.C
Public Domain

CHAPTER 11
COMING HOME

"In our darkest hour, God's light shines the Brightest"

DATELINE; LODZ,
POLAND - 1945

David realized there was little time to lose. Dora was on the verge of death and he had to take matters into his own hands. He assumed the doctor was not coming and somehow he had to find a way to get Dora to the main hospital in town, without delay. The infirmary did not have the personnel nor the equipment to handle this kind of an emergency. David turned to Sara, "Sara, try to keep Dora comfortable, I'm going downstairs to see what I can do to get Dora to the main hospital. I'm not waiting for the doctor to get here."

As he opened the door to the first floor, it was evident that the nurse on-call was too busy tending to her patients in order to provide any assistance. As he turned to see who else could help him, an Orderly approached him. "Can I help you Sir?". David replied, "Yes, my wife is falling into a coma on the second floor. Can you call an ambulance? It's urgent!" The Orderly replied, "The only ambulance we have is across town, and I'm not sure how long it will take the ambulance to get here. We have no vehicles available, but I'm sure the doctor will be here shortly."

David knew Dora was in a life or death situation. There was no time to wait for the doctor. Without hesitating, he grabbed the orderly by the arm and asked him to come outside. A light rain was falling as they walked down the stairs. "We have no time to lose" David said,

"My wife is dying, and we need to flag down a car and get her to the hospital right away!" The orderly looked puzzled for a moment, but followed David's orders, as they both walked toward the road. They both stepped onto the roadway to see if any vehicles were coming towards them. They saw nothing in either direction. It was Sunday and few vehicles were on the road. They waited several minutes, which seemed like an eternity. There were still no vehicles coming. The Orderly, walked further down the road to get a better view, suddenly he yelled, "Mr. Mr., I see a car coming!" David, his adrenaline pumping, turned and looked into the distance. Indeed a car was coming. He and the Orderly began waving their arms frantically, though the vehicle was still a distance away. As the car drew near, it slowed and pulled up towards the two men. The man inside the car rolled down his window, but before he could say a word, David began to speak. "My wife has fallen into a coma and she needs medical attention right away. Can you drive her to the main hospital?" The driver feeling David's desperation, responded "Yes, of course. I'm Dr. Berg. The nurse called earlier, but I was detained by an emergency in town." As the doctor pulled up to the entrance of the infirmary, David thought it was no coincidence that the first car spotted on the road was the doctor. Could that be a sign from God? He believed so.

As the three men entered the building and ascended to the second floor, David opened the door and saw Sara placing a wet washcloth on Dora's forehead, hoping to keep her raging fever under control. The doctor, now at Dora's side, quickly examined her and said in a calm but firm voice "we must get her to the car right away. We have no time to lose." With that, the three men and Sara lifted the cot and started carrying Dora down the stairs to the Doctor's car. The doctor gently lifted Dora and placed her on the back seat, asking David and the Orderly to sit with her, while Sara sat up front. David sat holding Dora's head against his shoulder, as the doctor accelerated quickly in the direction of the main hospital, as the car skidded along the wet roadway.

Once reaching the hospital's emergency door, two nurses ran out knowing there must be something seriously wrong, since the doctor rarely ever pulled up in front of the emergency room door. The almost comatose Dora was gently placed on a gurney and wheeled into the Intensive Care Unit. For the next hour David and Dora waited for Dr. Berg to examine Dora and give them an update to her condition. It seemed like and eternity. He finally entered the waiting room with a concerned look on his face. "I'm afraid Dora's condition is very serious. She is severely dehydrated and the bacteria has spread into her lymph nodes. The doctors and I believe she has a 50/50 chance of survival. The next few days will be critical and will do our best to keep her alive. I'm sorry we can't give you a better prognosis." David and Sara were devastated.

For the next few days, David and Sara remained in the ICU, keeping a watchful eye over their beloved Dora, praying for her recovery. Neither one slept much, each taking turns resting in an adjacent room, while the other watched over her. Dora was never left alone. She was given fluids and antibiotics around the clock by the medical staff. Very few words were spoken by David or Sara to the attending nurses. Mostly, they just prayed and waited.

By the end of the sixth day, Dora's condition turned. Her high fever broke. On day seven, Dora came out of her coma. David and Sara were jubilant to see her eyes finally open. She smiled, noticing them at her bedside. Sara began to weep. Dora, her voice weaken by her illness. **"David you are here"** She smiled and gently closed her eyes again. At that very moment the door opened. The nurse walked in to take Dora's vitals. After completing her tests, she remarked. "Quite an improvement from yesterday. I am sure the doctor will be pleased."

Later that morning, Dr. Berg arrived and entered Dora's room to examine her as he did from the first day she arrived. David and Sara stood in the hallway, anxiously waiting to hear the doctor's assessment. The examination didn't take long. The doctor came out of Dora's room and took David aside, with Sara standing a few feet behind him. "David, I'm glad to say that Dora has made a dramatic improvement since yesterday. We'll continue to keep a watchful eye on her for the next few days to see if her condition continues to improve. Barring any complications, I believe she has a good chance to make a full recovery." David and Sara were jubilant hearing the news and hugged. The doctor continued, "I must admit, the doctors and I were very concerned when she first arrived due to her weakened state and high temperature. All of us believed her chances of recovery were slim. Your wife is a very strong woman, David." The doctor paused for a moment, as he looked over his notes on his clipboard. "Frankly, her turnaround is rather remarkable." The doctor shook David's hand and smiled at Sara. As he began walking away, he turned to look at them with a slight grin, "You know, it wasn't entirely the antibiotics and respiratory that made the difference in her recovery. I believe the both of you were a big reason why she improved so much over the past several days." David and Sara smiled. They both knew God was there with them.

PHOTO:
Polish Hospital in Warsaw, Poland

PHOTO CREDIT:
This image (or other media file) is in the public domain because its copyright
has expired and its author is anonymous.

CHAPTER 12
A NEW DAY DAWNS

*"Give me your tired, your poor,
your huddled masses
yearning to breathe free."*

Emma Lazarus, 1883 on the Statue of Liberty

DATELINE:
FOEHRENWALD, GERMANY
AND NEW YORK CITY 1946

PHOTO SPREAD:
Immigrants on a ship approaching New York City, bound for Ellis Island, with the Statute of Liberty in the background.

PHOTO CREDIT:
Photo is in public domain. The work is in public domain in the United States because it was published (or registered with the U.S. Copyright Office before January 1, 1926. From Wiki media Commons, the free media repository. The work is in the public domain in the United States because it was published (or rgisteres with the U.S. Copyright Office before Januay1, 1926) From Wikimedia Commons, the fee media repository.

ew York, Ellis Island. weg. No. 3163E

PHOTO
Ellis Island Immigration Station, Ellis Island New York.

PHOTO CREDIT:
Public Domain

PHOTO:
Immigrants and Inspectors in the registry room for legal inspections at Ellis Island.

PHOTO CREDIT:
The conversion (online magazine). Michigan State University, Kristen Fermaglich, Associate Professor, Michigan State University. Creative Commons.
n. The
work is in the public domain in the United States because it was
published (or rgisteres with the U.S. Copyright Office before Januay1,
1926) From Wikimedia Commons,
the fee media repository.

PHOTO:
Dora Ruskin with her students in the Foehrenwald Displacement Camp, 1946. Bavaria, Germany. (Dora Far Right)

PHOTO CREDIT:
Yad Vashem, photo Archive, Jerusalem, Israel

PHOTO:
Allen (baby carriage)
foreground with U.N.
dignitaries and General
Dwight D. Eisenhower.

PHOTO CREDIT:
Ruskin Family Album

PHOTO:
General Dwight Eisenhower
visits the school and syngogue
during an offical tour of the
Neu Freimann displaced per-
sos camp. Mucnich, Germany
1945

PHOTO CREDIT:
United States Holocaust Memorial Museum
Provenance: Jack Sutin Photo 20347
Source Record ID: Collections 02684

CHAPTER 12
A NEW DAY DAWNS

"Give me your tired, your poor, your huddled masses yearning to breathe free."

Emma Lazarus, 1883 on the Statue of Liberty

DATELINE:
FOEHRENWALD, GERMANY
AND NEW YORK CITY 1946

With Dora's condition continuing to improve, she was able to leave the hospital within a few weeks. The couple settled into a one bedroom apartment in the Lodz Displacement camp, not far from the hospital. Within 6 months, Dora's feisty disposition had returned, and the couple decided to transfer to the Foehrenwald Displacement Camp, just south of Munich, Germany, in hopes of emigrating to a new home. The couple, and thousands of other displaced people had no interest returning to their home countries, where memories of their horrific past were still fresh in their minds. Besides, most of their homes had been devastated by the war or confiscated by the Russians after liberation. Further, Antisemitism continued to remain pervasive among the populous within a good percentage of European "Eastern Bloc" countries.

The Foehrenwald camp was one of the most recognized DP camps within the American Zone. (Central Europe). The facility housed nearly 5700 refugees from Germany, Poland,

Hungary and the Baltic countries. The camp was well-equipped with the latest conveniences, including indoor plumbing, appliances, and electricity. Truly a luxury for thousands who had survived such unimaginable living conditions during the war.

While in the Foehrenwald Camp, Dora, under UN charter guidelines, organized a small group of teachers to establish the first school for children and adults interested in taking classes in a variety of subjects including writing, reading, arithmetic, and social studies. Fluent in six languages, Dora was well-qualified to converse with most of her students representing many nationalities and backgrounds. She, along with other teachers, established the school's student enrollment, curriculum, schedules and classroom size. They also provided counseling services.

The senior administrators of the UN Relief Agency responsible for the overall welfare of the camp were pleased to see how effective the educational programs were being run by Dora and her staff at Foehrenwald. To show their appreciation for her and her staff's hard work and dedication to the students in 1946, Dora and her staff were honored at a special ceremony at the camp. Attending the ceremony were a number of U.N. dignitaries, government officials and military personnel including the honorable General Dwight D Eisenhower. General Eisenhower, who was the Commander of all U.S. troops in the European theater during World War II, later became the 32nd President of the United States. Expressing her gratitude and appreciation for being recognized for her service, Dora stated to the audience that "The children in the camp are gifts to the World from God. They will carry the legacy of their parents, which will bring us to a new day of peace and unity".

It so happened that in the same year, God blessed David and Dora with the birth of their first Son Chaim (Allen), named after Dora's late father who was killed during the Holocaust. For the next two years, Dora continued to teach, as the couple waited for exit visas to emigrate to another country, preferably the United States or South Africa since both David and Dora had relatives in both countries. In the meantime, Sara was able to obtain sponsorship through her husband's family (Sara met her husband in the Foehrenwald camp the previous year and immigrated to Israel, where she and her husband lived for the remainder of their lives).

In January 1949, after many months of corresponding with relatives and the emigration Service the couple finally received a letter from David's first cousin Aron who offered the family sponsorship to Johannesburg, South Africa, where David could work at his cousin's clothing factory in plant maintenance. They were elated by the news. During the same week, Dora received a letter from Uncle Max, her late father's brother, that he was accepted by the emigration Service as a sponsor and could sponsor the couple to come to New York City. The couple carefully considered both offers and decided that America would be their new home.

On May 14th, 1949, the Ruskins, along with their three-year-old son, set sail from Munich Germany to New York City, with 1,500 other refugees from various displacement camps throughout the Central Zone. The nine day voyage was long and difficult. The ship ran into rough seas and several storms, with many passengers becoming very ill. Dora was one of them. Fortunately she made it through the illness, although she spent most of the voyage in bed.

In late May, as the last rays of sunlight were quickly fading below the horizon of orange and yellow, the 1,500 passengers on board the ship got their first glimpse of America. As they looked out from the ship's upper deck they saw the welcoming arms of the Statue of Liberty, and the magnificence of the of New York City skyline. It was a site to behold. Many of the weary passengers began to weep in joy; some just stood in amazement at the grandeur of the tall skyscrapers and the vastness of the landscape. The "buzz" from the passengers could be heard throughout the ship. Dora, David and their three year old son watched in awe. To Dora the moment was surreal. She realized how blessed she and her family were to see this day. It was a moment neither Dora or David would ever forget.

As the ship docked at Ellis Island, there was a sense of anticipation that spread amongst the passengers, as they envisioned their new lives as American citizens. The War seemed so long ago now, and their future so promising. Most on-board had little money in their pockets, and many couldn't speak English, but they were all grateful to be alive and having the freedom to begin new lives in the United States of America, where opportunities could go as far as their dreams could take them.

After the ship docked, David, Dora and their son were processed through Customs. Beyond the Customs' gates stood Uncle Max and his wife Carol, waiting to greet them. Dora could hardly remember her Uncle, as she was only a little girl when Max immigrated to the United States from Lithuania before Hitler came to power. He had known, even back then, that staying in Lithuania would be dangerous, due to the turbulent events evolving in Germany at the time. (1)Max and Carol greeted the "New Arrivals" at the gate. There were tears of joy as Dora hugged her Uncle and Aunt, knowing she was with family again. That evening they spent reminiscing about family and friends and the bittersweet days in Lithuania.

After a few months of sharing the apartment in Brooklyn, New York with Uncle Max and his wife, Max arranged a meeting between David and a close friend who was a Production Manager at a large paint manufacturing company in New Jersey. It so happened that the Manager had a need for someone with an electrical maintenance background and David turned out to be the perfect candidate for the job. David was soon hired as the company's Assistant Plant Electrical Technician. Later that year, Dora and David celebrated their new home in America with a blessed event, the birth of their second son, Michael. The proud parents were overjoyed with a second son and Allen having a brother. With the added addition to the family and David's long commute to New Jersey each day, David and Dora decided to move to Perth Amboy, New Jersey, a "bedroom" community" outside of New York City, where David's commute was much shorter. Their first apartment was located on Eagle Ave. Quite an appropriate name for new immigrants who came to America.

CHAPTER 12: A NEW DAY DAWNS

As David continued working at the factory, he also began moonlighting nights as an electrician for residents and commercial businesses in the community. It wasn't long after he began moonlighting that he tapped into his more "creative side," designing and selling lighting fixtures from the basement of their apartment. David, a "high-energy" type, liked being kept busy and holding down 3 jobs was perfect for him. Life was good!

As David's side business grew, Dora continued to raise the two children, but also found a part-time job as a seamstress at a nearby clothing factory. As her English became more fluent, and knowing she was capable of doing more than sew, she soon left the factory to become a bookkeeper at a local bank. She rose to become head bookkeeper within several years and stayed with the bank until she retired years later.

By working hard and saving as much as they could over the next several years, the couple eventually bought a two-story, 4-unit apartment building which they rented out to three other families. They were now homeowners, but even though money was still tight, they decided to give the boys piano lessons. The children became quite good at the piano, playing for friends and family for almost 8 years. They also performed in front of large gathering at the Jewish Community Center in their home town when Allen was 9 and Michael was 6. They made quite an impression on the audience as they played a duet. As the years passed, the boys had enough of piano and turned to something they liked even more,…baseball…, at their parents' dismay.

In 1967, the couple and their two children moved to Colonia, New Jersey, where they bought their first single family home. This was truly an achievement for a couple who had persevered to live the "American Dream". They remained in New Jersey until 1985, when David had a mild heart attack and they decided to retired and move to Miami Beach, Florida. During those later years in Miami Beach, they would walk hand and hand on the beach after dinner and reminiscing about years past, their children and their new grandchild, Lauren. For David and Dora, their life together truly was an "amazing journey." They were guided by God to be together.

On June 21, 1989, David and Dora celebrated their 50th wedding anniversary at Temple Emanuel in Miami Beach, Florida. In front of a large gathering of congregates and family members, the couple stood alongside the Rabbi as they were honored for their 50 years of marriage and the vow they took in 1944. The Rabbi gave a brief summary of their incredible lives together and their "special bond" which began in 1939. It was a tribute to their courage, perseverance and love for each other along with their unwavering faith in God, that brought them to that glorious day in Miami Beach. Truly a testimony to the strength of the Human Spirit.

On September 17, 1993, David passed away in Miami Beach, Florida, with his children at his bedside. On August 4, 2001, Dora joined him. Together again, as they vowed they would, forever more...

PHOTO:
Dora Ruskin and David Ruskin

PHOTO CREDIT:
Ruskin Family Album

CHAPTER 12: A NEW DAY DAWNS

FOOTNOTES:

(1) While still in Lithuania in the early 1930's, Uncle Max did all he could to persuade his brother, Dora's father, to immigrate along with his family to the U.S. Max believed, even then, that Hitler's rise to power could very well place European Jews in peril. Hitler, who was then the Chancellor of Germany, was continuing to fan the flames of anti-Antisemitism among the German people, which was very unsettling to Jews and others throughout Europe. There was no saying what Hitler would do should he continue his threatening rhetoric against the Jews, while building his military strength. Soon, rumors began to spread in Lithuania and elsewhere that Jews walking the streets of Munich and Berlin were being sent to forced labor for collaborating against the German State, charges that were totally unsubstantiated. The news in Germany made little difference to Rabbi Kekst. He would not be swayed to leave his beloved congregation and Lithuania. And sadly, he could not be convinced by his brother, Max, that the Jews of Lithuania could be in harm's way, should Hitler come to power. Ultimately, The Rabbi's decision to remain in Lithuania proved to be disastrous, for it cost him his life and the lives of most of his family.

PHOTO:
Dora Ruskin and David Ruskin
with Sara and friend,
1947

PHOTO CREDIT:
Ruskin Family Album

AFTERWARD

I would like to end my book with a few words about my parents, through the eyes of their son. People would say they found my parents to be warm and friendly. They would always greet you with a smile, whether you were their best friend or meeting them for the first time. People felt a connection almost instantly, even though they had rather strong European accents and sometimes mispronounced words. Most people understood them perfectly.

When entering our home you would never escape from my Mother's clutches of bringing you into the kitchen to feed you! I would always tell my friends be ready to eat something when you arrive. No one ever left my house hungry, that is a fact! To my Mom, food was always her way to "connect" with people. I would imagine she learned that from my grand-parents. My parents had sort of "European charm" that people found quite endearing.

My parents did not come from wealth after the war, nor did they achieve wealth in their lifetime. They had qualities that were much more important. They showed love and kindness from within, and people could sense their authenticity. They were simply blue collar, hard-working people who were grateful to be alive and living the "American Dream."

I believe my brother and I gave them purpose. They raised us in a culturally-bound Jewish home in a middle-class neighborhood. And they made sure we had a good education, good morals, and were responsibility for our lives.

My parents also had other qualities that were greatly admired. In a nutshell, they were very resilient, strong, and determined. Qualities which proved essential for their survival during the War and helped them establish productive lives in America.

During my childhood, they spoke Yiddish (a Polish/German hybrid) in our home, but frequently spoke Hebrew between themselves, when discussing matters they didn't want my brother or me to know. In most instances it related to something we did or did not do. As parents they were not overly strict, but knew when to draw the line. I believe they did a pretty good job parenting, considering they had to raise two feisty American kids who frequently tested their patience.

Now, as I look back on my formative years in New Jersey, I really had a difficult time connecting to what my parents had gone through in Lithuania.

I'm not excusing myself for my insensitivity, but I was born in the United States, years after World War II. It was a different time, a different place, a different culture. Times in the United States were good in the 1950's, when the country was enjoying the "good life"! It seemed like everyone was buying their first home, a new car and listening to great music, called rock and roll (well, at least the kids did!). My generation, the Baby Boomers, was looking forward to an exciting, bright future. We weren't looking back to a time of death camps, genocide, and destruction which plunged the world into darkness. Further, my parents rarely spoke about those days, and for good reason. Why would they want to relive the nightmare from their past?

I still recall, in my early years, sitting in the living room with my parents watching documentaries on TV regarding World War II and the atrocities against the Jews. But for some reason, I never connected those horrific scenes to my parents. Maybe I just didn't want to know the suffering they had gone through. Or perhaps it was because they hardly spoke about their past and I couldn't make the connection. Now years later, I've come to realize how blessed I was to have them as my parents and what incredible Souls they were, indeed. To have endured so much for so long during one of the darkest chapters in human history, was nothing short of a miracle. They taught my brother and me to understand the importance of perseverance, courage, love and having faith. They set a good example for my brother and me to follow.

Now as the years quickly pass, I sometimes wonder if I lived up to their expectations. I certainly tried. But one thing I know for sure; my love and, respect for my parents will always remain strong. They gave me love and guidance to build a wonderful life. And I am deeply grateful. I can honestly say as their son, they were more than just my parents....

They are my **"Heroes!"**

TIME LINE

1938	1939	JUNE, 1941

David and Dora meet for the first time in Kaunas, Lithuania through Dora's sister Sara. The couple begin a courtship, fall in love and marry. The wedding takes place in Dora's home with her father, a Rabbi, conducting the wedding.

Couple move into their new apartment in Kaunas. She gives birth to her first child Rose Miriam. The Soviet Union and Germany agree on a non-aggression pact between the two countries. Germany violates pact and invades Poland to usher in World War II.

Germany invades and occupies Lithuania pushes Soviets back into Russian territory while occupying the country. All Jews are singled out as enemies of the State, accused of collaborating with the Russians, which was never substantiated. Many Jews are rounded up and executed while others are killed by the local militia who are fervent anti-Semites, pro-Nazi sympathizers. Jews are segregated and required to wear a Star of David on their clothes and limited to their movement around the city. Local Government is run by the Nazi overlords and administers harsh edicts towards the Jews.

TIME LINE

AUG.,1941	MARCH, 1944	JUNE, 1944

Germans establishes a designated area inside the city which all Jews must enter. Called the Kovno Ghetto, over 30,000 Jews including the couple and their daughter are forced to move from their homes and enter the ghetto which is tightly controlled by the Germans. Area is barbwired and guarded 24/7; food rations are limited. No one can leave the Ghetto other than those who are ordered into forced labor under extreme harsh conditions.

Nazi and Ukrainian SS raid homes in the Ghetto. The operation is called "Die KiderAKtion". Roughly 2,500 people which include 1,600 children and infants are taken from their homes and executed inside a execution facility (converted prison) on the outskirts of town. Rose was one of the children taken.

The Ghetto is converted to Kauen Concentration Camp and soon many are deported to Dachau and Stutthof CC, as the camp is being liquidated. David and Dora are deported to different camps, separated for the first time since marriage. They make a vow to return to Kaunas when the war ends. The trains depart, no passengers aboard either train know their final destination, the CC camps.

TIME LINE

| APRIL, MAY, 1945 | JUNE, JULY, 1946 | MAY, 1949 |

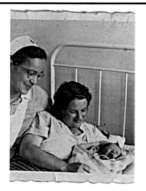

LIBERATION:
Daivd liberated by American forces, Dora liberated by Russian troops. After recuperating from his treatment in Dachau, David begins his mission to find his wife. Traveling through 4 countries and at a dozen cities and towns, he finds her. She is barely alive having contracted typhus and rushes her to the hospital.

After being reunited they move to a Displacement Camp in Germany where Dora and a group of teachers open up a school for children and adults who survive the war. She is recognized for her efforts as a special ceremony attended by General Dwight D. Eisenhower. She gives birth to her second child Allen.

The Ruskins and their three year old son Allen, set sail from Germany to New York City, along with 1500 other refugees. They arrive at Ellis Island, and settle in Brooklyn, New York. Their second son Michael is born. They all move to New Jersey several years later.

T I M E   L I N E

JUNE, 1989	SEPT., 1993	AUG., 2002

David and Dora Ruskin celebrated their 50th wedding anniversary at Temple Emmanuel in Miami Beach, Florida. The Rabbi and congregates honor the couple for the lives they lived together and their Vow in 1944.

David passes away
He was 78

Dora passes away
She was 84

The following figures of the <u>Federal Agency for Civic Education</u> (Germany) show the annihilation of the Jewish population of Europe by (pre-war) country as percentage points:

Country	Estimated Pre-War Jewish population	Estimated killed	Percent killed
Poland	3,400,000	3,000,000	88.25%
Soviet Union (excl. Baltic states)	3,000,000	1,000,000	33.3%
Romania	757,000	287,000	38%
Hungary	445,000	270,000	60.7%
Czechoslovakia	357,000	260,000	73%
Germany	500,000	165,000	33%
Lithuania	150,000	145,000	96.7%
Netherlands	140,000	102,000	72.9%
France	300,000	76,000	25.33%
Latvia	93,500	70,000	74.9%
Austria	206,000	65,000	31.5%
Yugoslavia	68,500	60,000	87.6%
Greece	70,000	58,800	84%

Page 150

Belgium	90,000	25,000	27.8%
Italy	46,000	7,500	16.3%
Luxembourg	3,600	1,200	33.3%
Estonia	4,300	1,000	23%
Norway	1,800	758	42.1%
Bulgaria	48,400	142	0.3%
Denmark	7,800	116	1.49%
Albania	200	100	50%
Finland	2,200	7	0.32%
Total	**9,689,500**	**5,594,623**	**57.74%**

TOTAL NUMBER OF CHILDREN WHO PERISHED DURING HOLOCAUST: 1.5 MILLION

Credit:

Federal Agency for Civil Education: Germany

https://creativecommons.org/licenses/by-sa/3.0/

DOCUMENTATION

Reparations for Jewish suffering during the Holocaust and reimbursement for Jewish property that was stolen by the Nazis was agreed up by the West German Government in the early 1950's. From 1953 to 1965, West Germany paid the State of Israel, Jewish survivors, and German refugees hundreds of millions of dollars in a symbolic attempt to make up for the crimes committed by the Nazis during the Holocaust.

In 1964, My Parents through their Attorney in New York City petitioned the courts in Munich, Germany for such reparations. In order to do so, my parents had to go through an extensive mental and physical examination by attending physicians. Once the examinations were completed, the Doctors had to submit their findings to my Parents' attorney in New York, along with my parents' testimony describing their personal experiences during the Holocaust and how such events continued to negativity impact their lives to the present day.

The information you are about to read were the initial drafts of their written testimonies and doctors' notes. The final submission was later revised, and forwarded to the German Courts for determination of their request for reparations, which were subsequently granted in 1966.

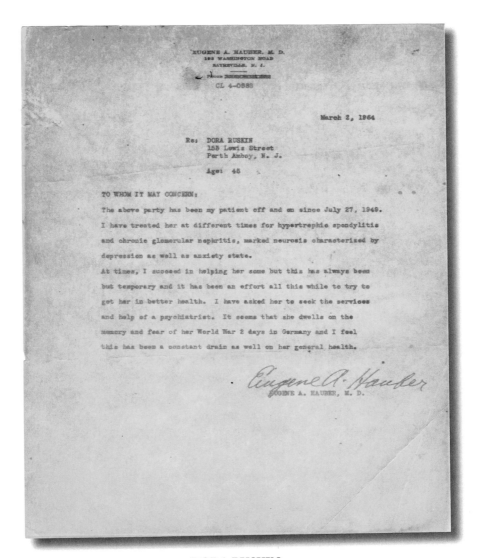

EUGENE A. HAUBER, M. D.
195 WASHINGTON ROAD
SAYREVILLE, N. J.
PHONE
CL 4-0886

March 2, 1964

Re: DORA RUSKIN
155 Lewis Street
Perth Amboy, N. J.

Age: 45

TO WHOM IT MAY CONCERN:

The above party has been my patient off and on since July 27, 1949.
I have treated her at different times for hypertrophic spondylitis
and chronic glomerular nephritis, marked neurosis characterized by
depression as well as anxiety state.

At times, I succeed in helping her some but this has always been
but temporary and it has been an effort all this while to try to
get her in better health. I have asked her to seek the services
and help of a psychiatrist. It seems that she dwells on the
memory and fear of her World War 2 days in Germany and I feel
this has been a constant drain as well on her general health.

Eugene A. Hauber
EUGENE A. HAUBER, M. D.

DORA RUSKIN:
Letter from Eugene A. Hauber, M.D., Sayreville, N.J.
March 2nd, 1964

Page 153

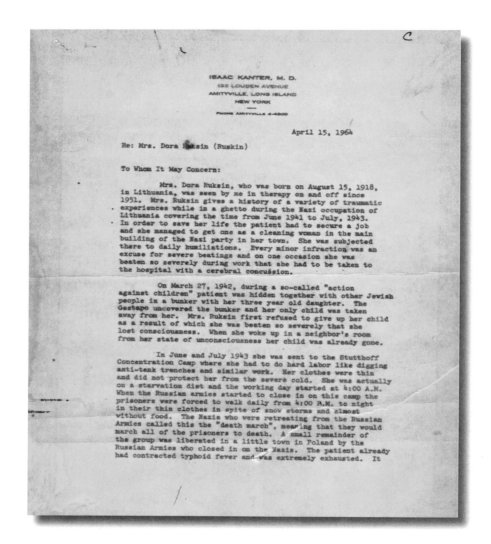

ISAAC KANTER, M. D.
125 LOUDEN AVENUE
AMITYVILLE, LONG ISLAND
NEW YORK
—
PHONE AMITYVILLE 4-4000

April 15, 1964

Re: Mrs. Dora Ruksin (Ruskin)

To Whom It May Concern:

Mrs. Dora Ruksin, who was born on August 15, 1918, in Lithuania, was seen by me in therapy on and off since 1951. Mrs. Ruksin gives a history of a variety of traumatic experiences while in a ghetto during the Nazi occupation of Lithuania covering the time from June 1941 to July, 1943. In order to save her life the patient had to secure a job and she managed to get one as a cleaning woman in the main building of the Nazi party in her town. She was subjected there to daily humiliations. Every minor infraction was an excuse for severe beatings and on one occasion she was beaten so severely during work that she had to be taken to the hospital with a cerebral concussion.

On March 27, 1942, during a so-called "action against children" patient was hidden together with other Jewish people in a bunker with her three year old daughter. The Gestapo uncovered the bunker and her only child was taken away from her. Mrs. Ruksin first refused to give up her child as a result of which she was beaten so severely that she lost consciousness. When she woke up in a neighbor's room from her state of unconsciousness her child was already gone.

In June and July 1943 she was sent to the Stutthoff Concentration Camp where she had to do hard labor like digging anti-tank trenches and similar work. Her clothes were thin and did not protect her from the severe cold. She was actually on a starvation diet and the working day started at 4:00 A.M. When the Russian armies started to close in on this camp the prisoners were forced to walk daily from 4:00 P.M. to night in their thin clothes in spite of snow storms and almost without food. The Nazis who were retreating from the Russian Armies called this the "death march", meaning that they would march all of the prisoners to death. A small remainder of the group was liberated in a little town in Poland by the Russian Armies who closed in on the Nazis. The patient already had contracted typhoid fever and was extremely exhausted. It

DORA RUSKIN
Letter from Dr. Issac Kanter M.D., Amityville, Long Island, NY
April 15, 1964 (Page One)

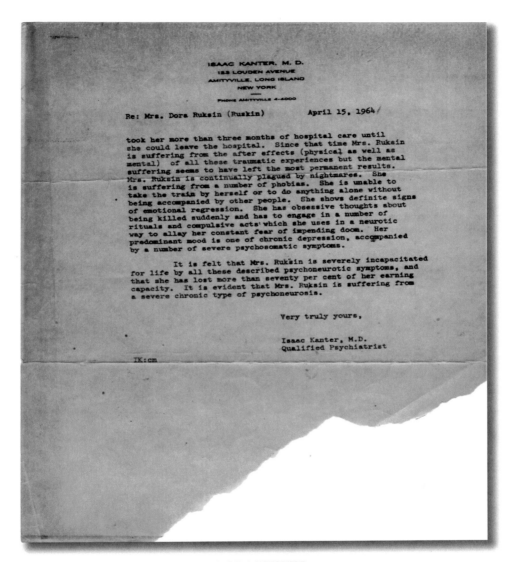

ISAAC KANTER, M. D.
123 LOUDEN AVENUE
AMITYVILLE, LONG ISLAND
NEW YORK
PHONE AMITYVILLE 4-4000

Re: Mrs. Dora Ruksin (Ruskin)   April 15, 1964

took her more than three months of hospital care until she could leave the hospital. Since that time Mrs. Ruskin is suffering from the after effects (physical as well as mental) of all these traumatic experiences but the mental suffering seems to have left the most permanent results. Mrs. Ruskin is continually plagued by nightmares. She is suffering from a number of phobias. She is unable to take the train by herself or to do anything alone without being accompanied by other people. She shows definite signs of emotional regression. She has obsessive thoughts about being killed suddenly and has to engage in a number of rituals and compulsive acts which she uses in a neurotic way to allay her constant fear of impending doom. Her predominant mood is one of chronic depression, accompanied by a number of severe psychosomatic symptoms.

It is felt that Mrs. Ruskin is severely incapacitated for life by all these described psychoneurotic symptoms, and that she has lost more than seventy per cent of her earning capacity. It is evident that Mrs. Ruskin is suffering from a severe chronic type of psychoneurosis.

Very truly yours,

Isaac Kanter, M.D.
Qualified Psychiatrist

IK:cm

DORA RUSKIN
Letter from Dr. Issac Kanter M.D., Amityville, Long Island, NY
April 15, 1964 (Page Two)

LOUIS F. GOULD, M. D.
95 MARKET STREET
PERTH AMBOY, N. J.
P. A. 4-0808

December 13, 1954

To Whom It May Concern:

Mr. David Ruskin of 164 Brighton Avenue, Perth
Amboy, New Jersey, has been under my care since January
15, 1952.

His complaint repeatedly center about pain in
the left anterior chest and left upper abdominal quadrant.
Physical exam including fluoroscopy of the chest and
electrocardiography has failed to produce specific evidence
of definite organic disease. It is felt that he is suffering from a deep seated Psychoneurosis with the presence,
probably, of a Radiculitis of the left 7th intercostal
nerve.

Very truly your,

Louis F. Gould

Louis F. Gould, M.D.

Subscribed and sworn to
before me the 22nd day of
December 1954

Wilbur T. Egan
Notary Public N.J.
COMMISSION EXPIRES
AUGUST 26, 1956

David Ruskin

DAVID RUSKIN:
Letter from Dr. Louis Gould, M.D., Perth Amboy, N.J.
December 13, 1954

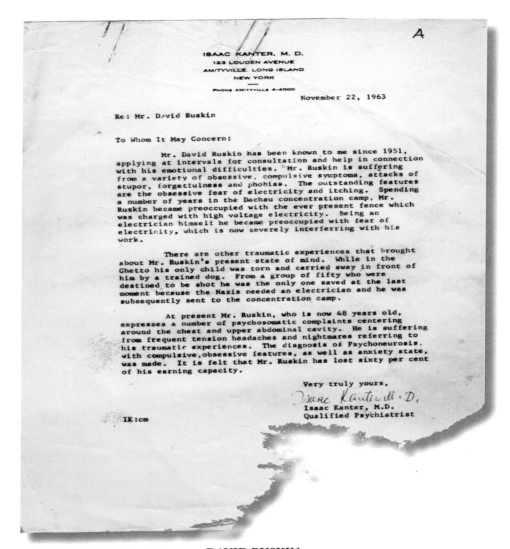

DAVID RUSKIN:
Letter from Dr. Issaac Kanter M.D., Amityville, Long Island, N.Y
November 22, 1963

EUGENE A. HAUBER, M. D.
195 WASHINGTON ROAD
SAYREVILLE, N. J.
PHONE SOUTH RIVER 888

March 2, 1964

Re: DAVID RUSKIN
       155 Lewis Street
       Perth Amboy, N. J.

       Age: 48

TO WHOM IT MAY CONCERN:

This party has been a patient of mine since May 19, 1949. I
first made contact with him by way of being plant physician
where he worked and have treated him off an on over the years
for chronic bronchitis, chronic and persistent sinusitis,
neuro-dermatitis and anxiety state.

He has been hospitalized several times over the years and has
lost some time from work due to the illnesses mentioned. His
absentee record has increased over the past year as it is
difficult to carry on his work in any sustained degree.

Since coming to this country from Germany in World War 2, he
has gained but 10 pounds and keeping up his health and nourishment has been a continuous task.

Eugene A. Hauber

EUGENE A. HAUBER, M. D.

DAVID RUSKIN:
Letter from Eugene A Hauber, M.D., Sayterville, N. J.
March 2, 1964

Exhibit D

STATE OF NEW JERSEY

COUNTY OF MIDDLESEX

I, Dora Ruksin (Ruskin), nee Kekst, being duly sworn according to law, on my oath depose and say that:

I reside at 155 Lewis Street, Perth Amboy New Jersey, and am a naturalized citizen of the United States of America.

I was born on August 15, 1918 in Mazeikiai, Lithuania. I lived in Kovna, Lithuania. In 1941 I entered the Kovna ghetto a healthy person. There I was forced to work as a cleaning lady in the Nazi Party House. One day I accidently damaged a desk in one of the Nazi offices. When I reported this to an officer he started beating me and he knocked out three of my teeth. He beat me until I was unconscious and when I woke up I was at the ghetto hospital. Since that horrible affair I have had dizzy spells often.

In 1943 the Nazis' took all Jewish children away from their mothers in order to have them killed. At this time I was hiding in a bunker with my little girl. A Nazi soldier found us and he grabed my little girl away from me. When I tried to run after my baby he knocked me out with his rifle. After this incident I was so griefstricken that I became very ill. It was and still is sort of an emotional illness.

In 1944 I was sent to Stutthof Concentration Camp. The Nazis' took from us all our personal possessions including our clothes. Then I was forced into hard labor by digging anti-tank ditches around Stutthof. Even in the bitter cold of winter, almost without any food or clothing I was forced to work. In

DORA RUSKIN:

Copy of page one of her Restitution Claim

Exhibit B

STATE OF NEW JERSEY

COUNTY OF MIDDLESEX

I, David Ruksin (Ruskin), being duly sworn according to law, on my oath depose and say that:

I reside at 155 Lewis Street, Perth Amboy, New Jersey, and am a naturalized citizen of the United States of America.

I was born May 27, 1915 in Kadainiai, Lithuania. In 1941 the Nazis took me to the Kovna lager where I was forced to work without pay or any sanitary working and living conditions. Many times I was beaten and forced to work 18 hours a day.

In the early months of 1942 the Nazis took 50 of my fellow workers to be shot. A note from the head of the Gestapo saved me. In the note it said that I should not be harmed because I was needed by the Nazis as an electrician. Nevertheless the Nazis made me watch as they shot down 50 of my best friends.

One day in 1944 I just came back from working when before my eyes I saw a trained Nazi dog take my little baby away from my wife while she screamed and tried to stop them. As long as I live I will never forget that horrible thing that the Nazis did to my wife and I.

In April of 1944 I was transfered to Schanch Concentration Camp. In June of 1944 I was sent to Dachau Concentration Camp where the conditions where horrible. I joined the electrical command where I worked for the Moil Company at Lagar 1 in Dachau. I was made to wear a striped prison uniform. The Nazis marched me 4 miles to work every day. I got up at 5 A.M. and got back at 9 P.M.. The only pay I got was a little horsemeat, bread and water. The conditions were so horrible the people comitted suicide

DAVID RUSKIN:
Copy his Restitution Claim No. 21267/VII/34848
Page 1

by jumping off scaffolds and on to electric fences. Sometimes I was forced to pull these people out of the fences and bury them. In that period I got so afraid of those electric fences that I became deathly afraid of electricity itself and now I can no longer work at my trade as an electrician. Those horrible incidents with the electric fences has now made me afraid to work at my trade as an electrician. I can still see those burned bodies in my mind. This period in my life has left a scar on my mind that I can't seem to get rid of. Many times I have nightmares and can't sleep when I think of the concentration camps and the things I had to suffer through. I wake up in a cold sweat many times. My children tell me that I scream at night in my sleep.

In April of 1945 the Nazis started to evacuate Dachau, lagar 1. I was forced to march day and night to the Troiol Mountains. On May 6, 1945 I was freed by the Americans. I was hospitalized in the city of Batells, Germany for a month. After this I was evacuated to Funk Kaserna, Munich.

Since that nightmare in my life I have never regained my standing as a really normal person. I have nightmares and break out in cold sweats. I very often scream in my sleep. I am afraid of electricity and so I can not work at my learned trade of an electrician. Since I have gotten my freedom I have constantly been under doctors care.

My Restitution Claim is registered in Munchen, number 21267/VII/34848.

Sworn and subscribed before me

this   day of   196   David Ruksin (Ruskin)

DAVID RUSKIN:
Copy his Restitution Claim No. 21267/VII/34848
Page 2

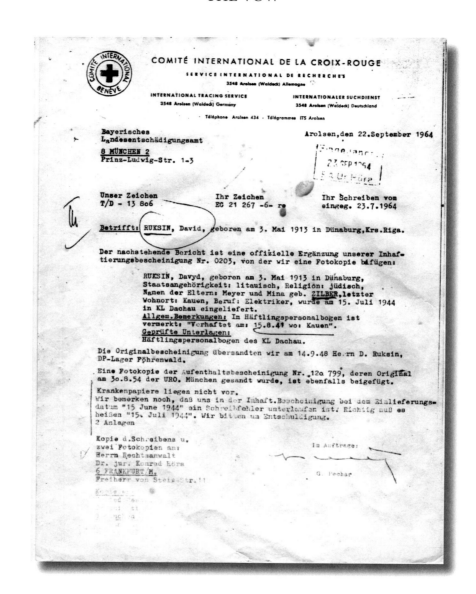

COMITÉ INTERNATIONAL DE LA CROIX-ROUGE
SERVICE INTERNATIONAL DE RECHERCHES
3548 Arolsen (Waldeck) Allemagne

INTERNATIONAL TRACING SERVICE   INTERNATIONALER SUCHDIENST
3548 Arolsen (Waldeck) Germany   3548 Arolsen (Waldeck) Deutschland

Téléphone Arolsen 434 · Télégrammes ITS Arolsen

Bayerisches   Arolsen,den 22.September 1964
Landesentschädigungsamt
8 MÜNCHEN 2
Prinz-Ludwig-Str. 1-3

Unser Zeichen   Ihr Zeichen   Ihr Schreiben vom
T/D - 13 806   EG 21 267 -6- re   eingeg. 23.7.1964

Betrifft: RUKSIN, David, geboren am 3. Mai 1913 in Dünaburg,Krs.Riga.

Der nachstehende Bericht ist eine offizielle Ergänzung unserer Inhaf-
tierungsbescheinigung Nr. 0203, von der wir eine Fotokopie beifügen:

      RUKSIN, Davyd, geboren am 3. Mai 1913 in Dünaburg,
      Staatsangehörigkeit: litauisch, Religion: jüdisch,
      Namen der Eltern: Meyer und Mina geb. ZILBER,letzter
      Wohnort: Kauen, Beruf: Elektriker, wurde am 15. Juli 1944
      in KL Dachau eingeliefert.
      Allgem.Bemerkungen: Im Häftlingspersonalbogen ist
      vermerkt: "Verhaftet am: 15.8.41 wo: Kauen".
      Geprüfte Unterlagen:
      Häftlingspersonalbogen des KL Dachau.

Die Originalbescheinigung übersandten wir am 14.9.48 Herrn D. Ruksin,
DP-Lager Föhrenwald.

Eine Fotokopie der Aufenthaltsbescheinigung Nr. 120 799, deren Original
am 30.8.54 der URO. München gesandt wurde, ist ebenfalls beigefügt.

Krankenpapiere liegen nicht vor.
Wir bemerken noch, daß uns in der Inhaft.Bescheinigung bei dem Einlieferungs-
datum "15 June 1944" ein Schreibfehler unterlaufen ist. Richtig muß es
heißen "15. Juli 1944". Wir bitten um Entschuldigung.
2 Anlagen

Kopie d.Schreibens u.
zwei Fotokopien an: Im Auftrage:
Herrn Rechtsanwalt
Dr. jur. Konrad Höra
6 FRANKFURT/M.
Freiherr von Stein-Str.11   G. Pechar

International Tracing Service Document
September 23, 1964

Telephone 51-1125.

Telegraphic Address:
"Silkcloth."

P.O. Box 274

South African Clothing Industries, Ltd.

Incorporating S. JACOBSON & SONS.

DIRECTORS:

GEORGE MACKENZIE
LEON JACOBSON } MANAGING
S. KRAMER
A. SILVER
L. FINGER

COR. PARK AND RAND ROADS,

Germiston, 13th January 12th November, 1948 1949

AFFIDAVIT.

I, the undersigned, ARON SILVER, residing at 58, Cachet Road, Germiston,

do hereby make oath and say:-

1. That I am a Director of the SOUTH AFRICAN CLOTHING INDUSTRIES LIMITED.

2. That DAVID RUKSIN of FOHRENWALD, who is making application to enter

 the Union of South Africa is my cousin.

3. That I am able to arrange for the employment of DAVID RUKSIN in

 the S.A. Clothing Industries Ltd. as an Electrical Mechanic at

 a salary of £45.0.0.d. per month and if required, can arrange for

 such employment to be for a fixed period.

4. That I am willing and able to assume financial responsibility for

 the maintenance and care of the said DAVID RUKSIN his wife DORA

 and child CHAIM in the Union.

5. That I can provide and am willing to provide for their living

 accommodation in my private house.

THUS DONE AND SWORN TO BEFORE ME at GERMISTON on this the 13th day of
November, 1949, by the deponent who acknowledges that he knows and understands
the contents hereof.

JUSTICE OF THE PEACE for
the District of Germiston,
COMMISSIONER OF OATHS

Immigration Request by Aron Silver for the Ruskins
to immigrate to South Africa 1949

Memorial Candle

ABOUT THE AUTHOR:

MICHAEL RUSKIN:
The Vow, a Love Story and the Holocaust

Michael Ruskin (born Meyer Ruksen), was born in Brooklyn, New York and raised in the beautiful city of Perth Amboy, New Jersey (central New Jersey). He is the youngest son of David and Dora Ruskin and the younger brother of Allen Ruskin. Michael is the last surviving member of his immediate family. A graduate from Kent State University in Ohio, he received a B.A. in Political Science and Psychology. Michael spent most of his 40 year career in corporate Human Resources and private consulting. Mr. Ruskin, now retired, lives a very active lifestyle which includes traveling, tennis, dancing, hiking, and biking. He is a student of spirituality, world history, and an avid researcher. He has one niece and enjoys spending time with friends and making new ones. The Vow, A Love Story and the Holocaust is Mr. Ruskin's first book, but not his last. He currently resides in Roswell, Georgia.

Michael Ruskin
THE VOW

A Love Story
and the Holocaust